A MANUAL FOR PRIESTS

A MANUAL FOR PRIESTS
OF THE
AMERICAN CHURCH

COMPLEMENTARY TO THE OCCASIONAL OFFICES OF THE BOOK OF COMMON PRAYER

Fifth Edition

Wipf & Stock
PUBLISHERS
Eugene, Oregon

Wipf and Stock Publishers
199 W 8th Ave, Suite 3
Eugene, OR 97401

A Manual for Priests of the American Church
Complimentary to the Occasional Offices of the Book of Common Prayer
By Maddux, Earle H.
ISBN: 1-59244-774-0
Publication date 7/27/2004
Previously published by Preservation Press, 1944

TO THE GLORY OF GOD

and in memory of
Those who taught me to love the Liturgy
CHARLES WINFRED DOUGLAS
Priest and Doctor of Music
and
NEIL EDMUND STANLEY
Priest and Bachelor of Laws

TABLE OF CONTENTS

APPENDIX

INDEXES

PREFACE

WHILE several excellent manuals of this sort have been produced in England, they did not entirely meet the needs of priests of the American Church. Moreover, these books did not always agree in text with the American Book of Common Prayer.

Few priests will have occasion to use every office and blessing in this book; but a deliberate attempt has been made to provide a manual of occasional offices and blessings which all the clergy may find useful in some degree, whether stationed in town or country, in the mission field, or with the armed forces.

Certain of the offices contained in this book are directly implied by the rubrics of the American Prayer Book and the Canons of the American Church. At the urgent request of many parish priests, a few offices from our own Prayer Book have been included. While materials have been freely drawn from Prayer Books of other Churches of the Anglican Communion, so far as possible these borrowings have been conformed to the text of the American Book of Common Prayer.

A few diocesan service books have been drawn upon; and a good many diocesan forms have been very carefully consulted. Many of the offices and blessings in this book have been widely used among us during the last hundred years. Blessings have been taken, and in some instances adapted, from contemporary Anglican sources; from those ancient Manuals which are part of our noble Anglican heritage; and, in the case of a few modern blessings, from the present Western Use. Collects and prayers have been drawn from many sources, including authorized Prayer Books of Churches of the Anglican Communion, the Sarum Missal, the Paris Missal, and various Office Books.

Directions for performing certain offices which may be unfamiliar to some have been set forth in unusual detail, in the hope that the usefulness of the book may be thereby increased.

The Occasional Offices and Prayers of the Prayer Book bear witness to the sovereignty of God: that he rules over the whole of life from birth to death, and that no concern of his children can be unimportant in his sight. This is in accord with the teaching of our Lord as recorded in the Gospels, and with the deepest convictions of the Church from earliest times. During recent years, discoveries in the realm of nature and of science have tended to dull man's perception of the overruling power of God; but for us as Christians there can be no department or activity of life from which God is shut out.

For the great needs and the great moments of life there are the seven Sacraments. But the lesser moments, the activities of daily life, these too are to be hallowed. Certain of the offices and blessings contained in this book are rightly concerned with the things of everyday life.

True, the blessing of growing crops will not take the place of a proper tilling of the soil; nor is the blessing of a sick child intended as a substitute for the services of a good physician! Yet both blessings are fitting recognitions of the sovereign power of God; and every priest who has faithfully and devoutly used such blessings in the course of his daily ministry knows from personal observation and experience that they are channels of God's grace and power.

Those who are familiar with other books of this kind will notice certain omissions in the present volume. It has not seemed necessary to provide special forms for the use of our Religious Communities, since each Community usually has its own proper services for the Reception of Novices, the Election of Superiors, and other similar occasions. Also, since this is a Manual for Priests, no provision has been made for those Offices and Blessings which are traditionally "reserved" to Bishops alone. The single exception is the form for the Consecration of a Chalice and Paten, which has been included in the Appendix at the request of many parish priests.

We are grateful to the late Reverend Canon Winfred Douglas for permission to reproduce texts appearing in *The Monastic Diurnal* and *The Saint Dunstan Kyrial;* to the Community of Saint Mary for permission to reprint translations from two copyrighted books privately printed for the use of that community; and to the Morehouse-Gorham Company of New York City, publishers of the first edition of *The American Missal,* for permission to use certain copyrighted translations made especially for the first edition of that work. No copyright has been wittingly violated; if the editor has inadvertently erred in that respect, he wishes to be promptly notified in order that suitable acknowledgment may be made in any subsequent edition of this book.

Those who are familiar with *Liturgy and Worship* will recognize our indebtedness to certain essays which appear in that valuable publication. *A Book of English Collects,* edited by the Very Reverend Doctor John W. Suter, Jr., has been a most useful manual of reference.

Thanks are due to the Reverend Doctor Edward R. Hardy, Jr., to the Reverend Paul Hartzell, and to the Reverend Meredith B. Wood, who have helped with wise counsel; to the good friends who have lightened the labour of proofreading; to Mr Donald Elliot of H. R. Elliot and Company, and the members of his staff, especially Mr John Rodgers, for their unfailing cooperative courtesy.

The editor owes a special debt of gratitude to the Reverend Mother Superior and the Sisters of the Convent of Saint Anne, Arlington Heights, Massachusetts, for extraordinary kindnesses extended throughout the period of the making of this book.

Especial thanks are due to the Reverend Father Williams, S.S.J.E., Superior of the American Congregation of the Society of Saint John the Evangelist, for his permission to undertake this work, and for his great kindness and consideration during its progress; to the Reverend Father McDonald, S.S.J.E., without whose inspiration and encouragement this book would never have been begun, nor brought to conclusion; to the Reverend Father Gibbs, S.S.J.E., and to Brother Martin, S.S.J.E., who have assisted in countless ways; and to all the other members of the American Congregation of the Society of Saint John the Evangelist who have helped with their interest, their patience, and their prayers.

EARLE HEWITT MADDUX, S.S.J.E.

Monastery of Saint Mary and Saint John, Cambridge
Feast of the Nativity of the B.V.M., 1944.

NOTE TO THE FIFTH EDITION

MANY have asked that a selection of occasional prayers be added to A MANUAL FOR PRIESTS. The request has been answered in this fifth edition by the provision of "Various Prayers" in the Appendix. Complementary to the American Prayer Book, these have been largely drawn, and in some instances modified, from the Scottish, Irish, Indian and South African Books of Common Prayer.

The prayer "For the Coming Year" has been taken from the Mozarabic Liturgy. "For a Birthday" was adapted from the American Prayer Book by the late Father Edward Everett, S.S.J.E. "For Explorers in Outer Space" is the work of four priests.

"The Blessing of a Stole" has been requested by very many. Shorter versions of the Candlemas and Ash Wednesday blessings have been substituted for the longer forms which have appeared hitherto. Other changes bring the book into line with current liturgical usage.

Special thanks are due to the Reverend Father Pedersen, S.S.J.E., Superior of the American Congregation of the Society of Saint John the Evangelist for his direction to bring out this edition. The Editor owes a particular debt of gratitude to The Reverend Mother Superior and the Sisters of All Saints Convent, Catonsville, Maryland, for many kindnesses extended throughout the preparation of this fifth edition. We are grateful to the clergy for their continuing interest and help.

Mr. A. A. Kajander, of The Riverside Press, has been most helpful in very many ways. To him and to his fellow-workers we are most grateful. Our deepest thanks to the generous friends who have lightened the labor of much proof reading!

EARLE HEWITT MADDUX, S.S.J.E.

All Saints Convent, Catonsville, Maryland
The Nativity of the B.V.M., 1968

PART I
OFFICES

PRIVATE BAPTISM

If possible, the Priest should wear a white stole.

¶ *When in consideration of extreme sickness, necessity may require, then the following form shall suffice:*

¶ *The Child (or Person) being named by some one who is present, the Minister shall pour water upon him, saying these words:*

N I baptize thee In the Name of the Father, and of the Son, and of the Holy Ghost. Amen.

¶ *Then shall be said,*

O UR Father, who art in heaven, Hallowed be thy Name. Thy kingdom come. Thy will be done, On earth as it is in heaven. Give us this day our daily bread. And forgive us our trespasses, As we forgive those who trespass against us. And lead us not into temptation, But deliver us from evil. For thine is the kingdom, and the power, and the glory, for ever and ever. Amen.

¶ *Then shall the Minister say,*

W E yield thee hearty thanks, most merciful Father, that it hath pleased thee to regenerate *this Child* (*this* thy *Servant*) with thy Holy Spirit, to receive *him* for thine own *Child*, and to incorporate *him* into thy holy Church. And humbly we beseech thee to grant, that *he*, being dead unto sin, may live unto righteousness, and being buried with Christ in his death, may also be *partaker* of his resurrection; so that finally, with the residue of thy holy Church, *he* may be *an inheritor* of thine everlasting kingdom; through Christ our Lord. *Amen.*

¶ *But* NOTE, *That in the case of an Adult, the Minister shall first ask the questions provided in this Office for the Baptism of Adults.*

3

DOST thou renounce the devil and all his works, the vain pomp and glory of the world, with all covetous desires of the same, and the sinful desires of the flesh, so that thou wilt not follow, nor be led by them?

Answer. I renounce them all; and, by God's help, will endeavour not to follow, nor be led by them.

Minister. Dost thou believe in Jesus the Christ, the Son of the Living God?

Answer. I do.

Minister. Dost thou accept him, and desire to follow him as thy Saviour and Lord?

Answer. I do.

Minister. Dost thou believe all the Articles of the Christian Faith, as contained in the Apostles' Creed?

Answer. I do.

Minister. Wilt thou be baptized in this Faith?

Answer. That is my desire.

Minister. Wilt thou then obediently keep God's holy will and commandments, and walk in the same all the days of thy life?

Answer. I will, by God's help.

¶ *In cases of extreme sickness, or any imminent peril, if a Minister cannot be procured, then any baptized person present may administer holy Baptism, using the foregoing form. Such Baptism shall be promptly reported to the Parish authorities.*

CONDITIONAL BAPTISM

¶ *If there be reasonable doubt whether any person was baptized with Water,* In the Name of the Father, and of the Son, and of the Holy Ghost, *(which are essential parts of Baptism), such person may be baptized in the form before appointed in this office; saving that, at the immersion or the pouring of water, the Minister shall use this form of words:*

IF thou art not already baptized, *N.*, I baptize thee In the Name of the Father, and of the Son, and of the Holy Ghost. Amen.

The Receiving of One Privately Baptized

See Rubric, page 281 of the Prayer Book

¶ *There shall be for every male child brought to be received into the Church, two Godfathers and one Godmother; and for every female, one Godfather and two Godmothers.*

¶ *When a child who has been privately baptized by some other person than the Priest is brought to be received into the Congregation, the Priest who receives the child shall satisfy himself that all has been well done, and according to due order, concerning the Baptism of the child; and shall, if need so require, examine those who bring the child to the church after this manner:*

BY whom was this child baptized?
Who was present when this child was baptized?
Because some things essential to this Sacrament may happen to be omitted through fear or haste, in such times of extremity; therefore I demand further of you,
Was this child baptized with water?
Was this child baptized with the form of words: I baptize thee In the Name of the Father, and of the Son, and of the Holy Ghost?

¶ *And if the Priest did himself baptize the child, or finds by the answers of those who bring the child that the child was baptized with water,* In the Name of the Father, and of the Son, and of the Holy Ghost; *then he shall not christen the child again; but, having inquired of the sponsors the name of the child, he shall receive him as one of the flock of true Christian people, saying thus:*

I CERTIFY you, that in this case all has been well done, and according to due order, concerning the baptizing of *this child*, *N.*; who, being born in original sin, *has* by the laver of regeneration in Baptism, been received into the number of the children of God, and heirs of everlasting life: for our Lord Jesus Christ does not deny his grace and mercy unto such infants, but most lovingly calls them unto him, as the Holy Gospel witnesses unto us to our comfort on this wise.

The Priest, vested in surplice and violet stole, having come near to the Font, shall say, (the People all standing):

℣. The Lord be with you.
℟. And with thy spirit.

Hear ✠ the words ✠ of the Gospel ✠, written by Saint Mark, in the tenth Chapter, at the thirteenth Verse.

℟. Glory be to thee, O Lord.

THEY brought young children to Christ, that he should touch them: and his disciples rebuked those that brought them. But when Jesus saw it, he was much displeased, and said unto them, Suffer the little children to come unto me, and forbid them not: for of such is the kingdom of God. Verily I say unto you, Whosoever shall not receive the kingdom of God as a little child, he shall not enter therein. And he took them up in his arms, put his hands upon them, and blessed them.

℟. Praise be to thee, O Christ.

Or this.

℣. The Lord be with you.
℞. And with thy spirit.

Hear ✠ the words ✠ of the Gospel ✠, written by Saint John, in the third Chapter, at the first Verse.

℞. Glory be to thee, O Lord.

THERE was a man of the Pharisees, named Nicodemus, a ruler of the Jews: the same came to Jesus by night, and said unto him, Rabbi, we know that thou art a teacher come from God: for no man can do these miracles that thou doest, except God be with him. Jesus answered and said unto him, Verily, verily, I say unto thee, Except a man be born again, he cannot see the kingdom of God. Nicodemus saith unto him, How can a man be born when he is old? can he enter the second time into his mother's womb, and be born? Jesus answered, Verily, verily, I say unto thee, Except a man be born of water and of the Spirit, he cannot enter into the kingdom of God. That which is born of the flesh is flesh; and that which is born of the Spirit is spirit. Marvel not that I said unto thee, Ye must be born again. The wind bloweth where it listeth, and thou hearest the sound thereof, but canst not tell whence it cometh, and whither it goeth: so is every one that is born of the Spirit.

℞. Praise be to thee, O Christ.

Or this.

℣. The Lord be with you.
℞. And with thy spirit.

Hear ✠ the words ✠ of the Gospel ✠, written by Saint Matthew, in the twenty-eighth Chapter, at the eighteenth Verse.

℞. Glory be to thee, O Lord.

JESUS came and spake unto them, saying, All power is given unto me in heaven and in earth. Go ye therefore, and make disciples of all nations, baptizing them in the name of the Father, and of the Son, and of the Holy Ghost: teaching them to observe all things whatsoever I have commanded you: and, lo, I am with you alway, even unto the end of the world.

℞. Praise be to thee, O Christ.

When the Office is used for a child, the Priest shall speak unto the Godparents on this wise.

DOST thou, in the name of this Child, renounce the devil and all his works, the vain pomp and glory of the world, with all covetous desires of the same, and the sinful desires of the flesh, so that thou wilt not follow, nor be led by them?

Answer. I renounce them all; and, by God's help, will endeavour not to follow, nor be led by them.

According to ancient custom, the Priest here anoints the Child with the Oil of the Catechumens, on the breast (at the base of the neck) and on the back between the shoulders, in the form of a Cross, saying once only:

I anoint thee with the Oil ✠ of salvation, in Christ ✠ Jesus our Lord, that thou mayest have eternal life.

The Priest then changes his violet stole for a white one, and continues:

Priest. **Dost thou believe all the Articles of the Christian Faith, as contained in the Apostles' Creed?**
Answer. **I do.**

Priest. **Wilt thou then obediently keep God's holy will and commandments, and walk in the same all the days of thy life?**
Answer. **I will, by God's help.**

Priest. **Having now, in the name of this Child, made these promises, wilt thou also on thy part take heed that this Child learn the Creed, the Lord's Prayer, and the Ten Commandments, and all other things which a Christian ought to know and believe to his soul's health?**
Answer. **I will, by God's help.**

Priest. **Wilt thou take heed that this Child, so soon as sufficiently instructed, be brought to the Bishop to be confirmed by him?**
Answer. **I will, God being my helper.**

When the Office is used for an Adult, the Priest shall address him on this wise, the Person answering the questions for himself.

DOST **thou renounce the devil and all his works, the vain pomp and glory of the world, with all covetous desires of the same, and the sinful desires of the flesh, so that thou wilt not follow, nor be led by them?**
Answer. **I renounce them all; and, by God's help, will endeavour not to follow, nor be led by them.**

Here the Priest may anoint the Person with the Oil of the Catechumens on the breast, and on the back between the shoulders, in the form of a cross, saying once only:

I anoint thee with the Oil ✠ of salvation, in Christ ✠ Jesus our Lord, that thou mayest have eternal life.

The Priest then changes his violet stole for a white one, and continues:

Priest. Dost thou believe in Jesus the Christ, the Son of the Living God?

Answer. I do.

Priest. Dost thou accept him, and desire to follow him as thy Saviour and Lord?

Answer. I do.

Priest. Dost thou believe all the Articles of the Christian Faith, as contained in the Apostles' Creed?

Answer. I do.

Priest. Wilt thou then obediently keep God's holy will and commandments, and walk in the same all the days of thy life?

Answer. I will, by God's help.

Then the Priest shall say,

WE receive this Child (Person) into the congregation of Christ's flock; and do ★ sign *him* with the sign of the Cross, in token that hereafter *he* shall not be ashamed to confess the faith of Christ crucified, and manfully to fight under his banner,

★ *Here the Priest shall make a Cross upon the Child's (or Person's) forehead, (using the holy Chrism, if desired)*

against sin, the world, and the devil; and to continue Christ's faithful soldier and servant unto *his* life's end. Amen.

Or, having signed the Child or Person with the Cross in the usual manner, the Priest may then anoint him *upon the crown of the head with the holy Chrism, saying,*

ALMIGHTY God, the Father of our Lord Jesus Christ, who hath regenerated thee by Water and the Holy Ghost, and hath given unto thee remission of all thy sins, vouchsafe to an✝oint thee with the Unction of his Holy Spirit, and bring thee to the inheritance of everlasting life. *Amen.*

If it is so desired, the Priest shall put upon the child *the white vesture commonly called the Chrysom, saying,*

WE give this white vesture, for a token of the innocency bestowed upon thee, and for a sign whereby thou art admonished to give thyself to pureness of living, that after this transitory life thou mayest be partaker of the life everlasting. *Amen.*

Then the Priest may give him *a lighted candle, (in the case of an Infant, the candle should be given to the Godfather), saying,*

RECEIVE the light of Christ, that when the bridegroom cometh thou mayest go forth with all the Saints to meet him; and see that thou keep the grace of thy Baptism. *Amen.*

Then shall the Priest say,

SEEING now, dearly beloved brethren, that *this Child* (*this Person*) *is* regenerate, and grafted into the body of Christ's Church, let us give thanks unto Almighty God for these benefits; and with one accord make our prayers unto him, that *this Child* (*this Person*) may lead the rest of *his* life according to this beginning.

Then shall be said,

OUR Father, who art in heaven, Hallowed be thy Name. Thy kingdom come. Thy will be done, On earth as it is in heaven. Give us this day our daily bread. And forgive us our trespasses, As we forgive those who trespass against us. And lead us not into temptation, But deliver us from evil. For thine is the kingdom, and the power, and the glory, for ever and ever. Amen.

Then shall the Priest say,

WE yield thee hearty thanks, most merciful Father, that it hath pleased thee to regenerate *this Child* (*this* thy *Servant*) with thy Holy Spirit, to receive *him* for thine own *Child*, and to incorporate *him* into thy holy Church. And humbly we beseech thee to grant, that *he*, being dead unto sin, may live unto righteousness, and being buried with Christ in his death, may also be *partaker* of his resurrection; so that finally, with the residue of thy holy Church, *he* may be *an inheritor* of thine everlasting kingdom; through Christ our Lord. *Amen.*

Then the Priest shall add,

THE Almighty God, the Father of our Lord Jesus Christ, of whom the whole family in heaven and earth is named; Grant you to be strengthened with might by his Spirit in the inner man; that, Christ dwelling in your hearts by faith, ye may be filled with all the fulness of God. *Amen.*

It is fitting that an adult who has been validly baptized by some one not a Priest or Deacon, before he receives other sacraments should come into the church with his Godparents, that the rites and ceremonies which were omitted at his Baptism may be there supplied.

Note: The ceremonies suggested in this Office have come down to us from the earliest ages. The form for the anointing with the Oil of the Catechumens is taken from the York Manual; that for anointing with the holy Chrism from the First Prayer Book of Edward VI. The forms for the giving of the Chrysom and the lighted candle are supplied from the Occasional Offices of the Church of the Province of South Africa. The use of the holy Chrism at "We receive this *child*" was suggested by the English Church Union at the time of the last revision of the English Prayer Book. The introduction to this office is taken from the Occasional Offices of the Church of the Province of South Africa.

Form of Admitting Catechumens

Adapted from the Occasional Offices of the
Church of the Province of South Africa

¶ *On the day appointed, the persons to be received*
shall be brought by their Godparents to the Church,
and shall remain in the Porch, or nigh unto the
Entrance, until the First Lesson of the Daily Office
is ended.

¶ *Then the Priest (or the Bishop, being present) shall*
go down to the Porch or place appointed for Catechu-
mens, and, those who are to be received being placed
in order nigh unto the Entrance of the Church, the
males on the right hand, the females on the left, he
shall demand of them as follows:

Minister. **What dost thou desire of God in his**
holy Church?
Answer. **Faith.**

Minister. **What does Faith gain for thee?**
Answer. **Eternal Life.**

Minister. **If thou wilt enter into life, keep the**
Commandments. Thou shalt love the Lord thy God
with all thy heart, and with all thy soul, and with all
thy mind, and thy neighbour as thyself. Moreover,
the right faith is that thou worship One God in
Trinity, and Trinity in Unity.

¶ *And again he demands:*

Dost thou renounce the Devil?
Answer. **I renounce him.**

Minister. **Dost thou believe in the One living and**
true God?
Answer. **I believe; Lord, help thou mine unbelief.**

Minister. **Wilt thou be further instructed in the**
Faith of Christ?
Answer. **I will.**

15

¶ *Then shall the Minister say,*

Peace be with thee.
Answer. **And with thy spirit.**

¶ *Then shall they kneel and the Minister shall say over them:*

O LORD God of Hosts, before the terrors of whose presence the armies of Hell are put to flight; Deliver these thy servants from the might of Satan; cast out from them every evil and unclean spirit that lurkest in the heart, the spirit of error and wickedness, the spirit of lying and all uncleanness, and make them meet to receive the Holy Spirit of grace; through Jesus Christ our Lord. *Amen.*

¶ *Then the Minister shall sign each one on the forehead in the form of a Cross, saying,*

Receive the Cross of Christ in thine heart.

¶ *And, when all are signed, he shall proceed:*

TAKE unto you the faith; keep the heavenly precepts; so live that you may be worthy to become the temples of the Holy Ghost, and, having entered into the Church of the living God, may rejoice that you have escaped the snares of death. Reject idolatry, heresy, and superstition; and worship God the Father Almighty, and Jesus Christ his only Son our Lord, who shall come to judge the quick and the dead.

Let us pray.

O LORD, our Heavenly Father, Almighty, everlasting God, who givest light to them that sit in darkness and in the shadow of death, lift up, we beseech thee, the light of thy countenance upon these thy servants who are wandering uncertain and doubtful in the night of this world; Make known unto them the way of truth and peace, and open the eyes of their understanding that they may walk therein; enable them to acknowledge thee, One God, the Father in the Son, and the Son in the Father, with the Holy Spirit, and keep them stedfast in this faith, that, loyally serving thee in this life, they may receive thy blessing in the life to come, through Jesus Christ our Lord. *Amen.*

O ALMIGHTY and merciful Father, who hast made all mankind, and dost restore through grace that which was lost by the infirmity of nature; Mercifully behold these thy servants, and let their names be written in the Book of Life, that, being defended by thy mercy, they may attain unto the glory of regeneration, and, receiving the fulness of thy grace, may be numbered amongst the children of the promise, through Jesus Christ, thine only Son our Lord, who through death hath destroyed death, and opened unto us the gate of everlasting life, to whom, with thee and the Holy Ghost, be all honour and glory, world without end. *Amen.*

¶ *Then shall each one bow down his head, and the Minister, laying his hand on the head of each severally, shall say,*

In the Name of the Lord.

¶ *And having so done, he prays as follows:*

Let us pray.

O HOLY Lord, Father Almighty, Everlasting God, who hast been from all eternity, and abidest unto the end; We humbly beseech thee for these thy servants whom thou hast called from the errors of the heathen, and from the shameful deeds of this world, that, being cleansed from the pollution of sin, and being regenerated by water and the Holy Spirit, they may put off the old man and put on the new, which according to thee is created in righteousness and true holiness, through Jesus Christ our Lord. *Amen.*

¶ *Then, the Catechumens all kneeling, the Priest (or Bishop being present) shall bless them on this wise:*

ALMIGHTY God, who hath called you to the knowledge of his grace, grant you an entrance into his kingdom, through Jesus Christ. *Amen.*

¶ *Adding this:*

THE Lord bless you and keep you: the Lord make his face to shine upon you, and be gracious unto you: the Lord lift up his countenance upon you, and give you peace, now and evermore. *Amen.*

¶ *Then let their names be inscribed in the Church Roll.*

Prayers Before Hearing Confessions

These may be said according to the opportunity of the Priest.

O LORD Jesus, I desire to administer this Sacrament of Penance with that same surpassing love with which thou didst hallow this ordinance, when with most earnest desire for our salvation thou didst institute it, to be administered by the Apostles and their successors, to the praise of God the Father, and the salvation of all mankind: I beseech thee that it may profit me, and all and each unto whom I shall minister it, in union with that love of thine, to the increase of our salvation, and of our everlasting happiness. Let the grace of the Holy Spirit so enlighten and kindle my senses and my heart, that according to thy good pleasure I may fulfil the ministry laid upon me, and may be counted worthy to be defended and preserved from every assault of temptation; In the Name of the Father, and of the ✠ Son, and of the Holy Ghost. Amen.

GRANT me, O Lord, the wisdom that sitteth at thy right hand, that I may judge thy people according to the right, and the poor with equity. Grant that I may so wield the keys of the Kingdom of Heaven, that I may open to none to whom it should be shut, nor shut it to any to whom it should be opened. Give purity to my intention, sincerity to my zeal, patience to my charity, and fruit to my labors. Grant that I may be mild, yet not remiss, stern, yet not cruel. Let me neither despise the poor nor flatter the rich. Give me gentleness to draw sinners unto thee, prudence in examination, wisdom in instruction. Grant me, I pray thee, skill to turn men aside from evil, perseverance to confirm them in good, zeal to persuade them to better things:

give wisdom to my answers, rightness to my counsels: give me light in darkness, a good understanding in confusion, victory in difficulties. Let no vain conversations entangle me, nor evil defile me: let me save others and not myself be cast away. Amen.

O LORD Jesus Christ, who didst say to thine Apostles, Whosesoever sins ye remit, they are remitted unto them; and whosesoever sins ye retain they are retained: look mercifully upon me thy servant; enlighten my understanding, give me a right judgement in all things, fill my heart with divine love. Grant me so to minister this thy gift of Absolution, that the hearts of these thy children may be truly turned to thee, that together with them I may attain to everlasting life. Who livest and reignest, world without end. Amen.

THE MANNER OF HEARING CONFESSIONS

Confessions ought always to be heard in the Church proper, except in cases of necessity or grave inconvenience. The Priest is ordinarily vested in surplice and violet stole; out of the Church building, he should at least wear a stole. In case of emergency, he may hear confessions in any garb.

Urged by any grave necessity, as in the peril of death, the Priest may briefly say:

I ABSOLVE thee from all thy sins, In the Name of the Father, and of the ✠ Son, and of the Holy Ghost. Amen.

The usual manner of administering the Sacrament of Penance is as follows:

The Priest, vested in surplice and violet stole, sits in the accustomed place where confessions are heard. The penitent, kneeling beside him, says in a low tone:

Bless me, Father, for I have sinned.

The Priest responds:

THE Lord be in thy heart and upon thy lips, that so thou mayest worthily confess all thy sins; In the Name of the Father, and of the ✠ Son, and of the Holy Ghost. Amen.

The penitent then makes his Confession, using the following or a similar formula:

I CONFESS to Almighty God, to all the Saints, and to you, Father, that I have sinned very much, in thought, word, deed, and omission, by my own great fault. Since my last confession which was (*here he tells the Priest when it occurred*), when I

21

received absolution and performed my penance, I have committed these sins:

He confesses his sins and continues:

For these and all my other sins which I cannot now remember, I am very sorry. I will try to do better, and I humbly ask pardon of God; and of you Father, I ask for penance, advice and absolution. Amen.

If it be a first confession, the penitent may say:

I CONFESS to Almighty God, to all the Saints, and to you, Father, that I have sinned very much, in thought, word, deed, and omission, by my own great fault. I have committed these sins:

He confesses his sins, and continues:

For these and all my other sins which I cannot now remember, I am very sorry. I will try to do better, and I humbly ask pardon of God; and of you Father, I ask for penance, advice and absolution. Amen.

After the Confession is ended, the Priest may address a few words of counsel to the penitent, and will then assign a suitable penance. For secret sins, however grave, public penance must not be imposed, lest the Seal of the Confessional be violated thereby.

Penance having been enjoined and accepted, the Priest shall say

THE FORM OF ABSOLUTION

ALMIGHTY God have mercy upon thee, forgive thee thy sins, and bring thee to everlasting life. Amen.

Then, raising his right hand toward the penitent, but not so as to be seen by anyone in the church, he continues:

THE Almighty and merciful Lord grant thee pardon, ✠ absolution, and remission of thy sins. Amen.

OUR Lord Jesus Christ, who hath left power to his Church to absolve all sinners who truly repent and believe in him, of his great mercy forgive thee thine offences: And by his authority committed unto me, I absolve thee from all thy sins, In the Name of the Father, and of the ✠ Son, and of the Holy Ghost. Amen. [*From the English Prayer Book*]

MAY the Passion of our Lord Jesus Christ make whatsoever good thou hast done, or evil thou hast endured, be unto thee for the forgiveness of sins, the increase of grace, and the reward of eternal life: And the blessing of God Almighty, the Father, the ✠ Son, and the Holy Ghost, be upon thee and remain with thee always. *Amen.*
Go in peace, the Lord hath put away all thy sins.

For reasonable cause, the foregoing prayers may be omitted, and only the Absolution Our Lord Jesus Christ, who hath left power, *need be said.*

When there are many to be confessed, it may be well to have the faithful instructed to say the whole of the preparatory form before approaching the confessional, and then, as soon as the Priest has given the usual blessing to begin by saying,

Since my last confession, which was, *etc.*

In some places, this version of the fourth paragraph of the form of Absolution is in use:

THE Passion of our Lord Jesus Christ, the merits of his holy Mother the blessed Virgin Mary, and of all the Saints, whatsoever good thou hast done, or evil thou hast endured, be unto thee for the forgiveness of sins, the increase of grace, and the reward of eternal life: And the blessing of God Almighty, the Father, the ✠ Son, and the Holy Ghost, be upon thee and remain with thee always. *Amen.*

A Prayer After Hearing Confessions

This may be said according to the opportunity of the Priest.

O LORD Jesus Christ, Son of the living God, accept this my ministry and service, with that exceeding love wherewith thou didst absolve blessed Mary Magdalene, and all sinners who fled unto thee. And whatsoever I have done carelessly or unworthily in the administration of this Sacrament, do thou be pleased to supply and to make satisfaction for by thyself. I commend to thy most loving Heart all and each who have now confessed unto me, beseeching thee to keep them, to preserve them from backsliding, and after the trials of this life to lead them to everlasting gladness with thee. Amen.

The Reception of Converts

See Rubric, page 299 of the Prayer Book

The manner of receiving an adult into this Church depends upon the group to which he belongs, as follows:

I *The unbaptized are received by the administration of the Sacrament of Baptism. The doubtfully baptized should receive Conditional Baptism before being admitted to the other Sacraments, and are formally received into the Church through that ministration.*

II *Those who have been validly baptized by some one not a Bishop, Priest or Deacon, before they receive other Sacraments, should come into the Church with their Godparents, that the rites and ceremonies which were omitted at their Baptism may be there supplied. See the Office on page 6.*

III *In the reception to the Communion of this Church of lay-persons who have already received the Sacrament of Confirmation in some other branch of the Holy Catholic Church, local or diocesan custom should be followed as to whether there should be any formal ceremony or not.*

If such persons have shared in the instruction given to candidates for confirmation, they may be properly blessed by the Bishop, and by him admitted to Communion; but it should be made clear that the Sacrament of Confirmation is not being repeated.

Where a service of reception by the parish Priest, or other Priest designated by the Bishop, is desired, the following may be used:

IN the Name of the Father, and of the ✠ Son, and of the Holy Ghost. Amen.

Let us pray.

DIRECT us, O Lord, in all our doings, with thy most gracious favour, and further us with thy continual help; that in all our works begun, continued, and ended in thee, we may glorify thy holy Name, and finally, by thy mercy, obtain everlasting life; through Jesus Christ our Lord. *Amen.*

Addressing the candidate the Priest shall say,

DO you solemnly declare that you have been duly baptized with water, in the Name of the Father, and of the Son, and of the Holy Ghost? *Answer.* I do.

Priest. Do you solemnly declare that you have received Confirmation in the Holy Catholic Church? *Answer.* I do.

Priest. Do you believe all the Articles of the Christian Faith, as contained in the Apostles' Creed? *Answer.* I do.

Priest. Do you desire to be received into the communion of this Church, as into a true part of Christ's Holy Catholic Church? *Answer.* I do.

Priest. Do you promise conformity to the doctrine, discipline, and worship of this Church? *Answer.* I do.

Then shall the Priest say to the candidate,

I RECEIVE and admit you into the communion of this Church, In the Name of the Father, and of the ✠ Son, and of the Holy Ghost. Amen.

Let us pray.

Lord, have mercy upon us.

Christ, have mercy upon us.

Lord, have mercy upon us.

OUR Father, who art in heaven, Hallowed be thy Name. Thy kingdom come. Thy will be done, On earth as it is in heaven. Give us this day our daily bread. And forgive us our trespasses, As we forgive those who trespass against us. And lead us not into temptation, But deliver us from evil. Amen.

O ALMIGHTY Lord, and everlasting God, vouchsafe, we beseech thee, to direct, sanctify, and govern, both our hearts and bodies, in the ways of thy laws, and in the works of thy commandments; that, through thy most mighty protection, both here and ever, we may be preserved in body and soul; through our Lord and Saviour Jesus Christ. *Amen.*

And the Priest shall bless him *saying,*

THE Blessing of God Almighty, the Father, the ✠ Son, and the Holy Ghost, be upon you, and remain with you for ever. *Amen.*

HOLY COMMUNION FROM THE RESERVED SACRAMENT

From time to time the Priest may be called upon to give Holy Communion to the faithful, in the Church and apart from the Mass. For example, communicants living far from the Church may be detained on the way, arriving in Church after Mass is over, and not be able to come again for a long period. Or, under present-day working conditions, it often happens that communicants are unable to get to Church at the hours when Mass is said.

In order that such communicants be not deprived of the Blessed Sacrament, the Priest may, if they are in a state of grace, give them Holy Communion in the Church and apart from Mass.

In some places it is customary to keep a burse containing a corporal always by the tabernacle; a small vessel of clean water and a purificator should also be by the tabernacle.

Under no circumstances should the tabernacle key ever be left in the Church; carelessness in this matter may result in the gravest sacrilege. The keys to the tabernacle ought always to be in the custody of the Priests of the Church.

When Holy Communion is to be given apart from Mass, two candles are lighted upon the Altar. The Priest washes his hands and vests in surplice and stole of the color of the day. On All Souls' Day he wears violet instead of black. If the burse is not already on the Altar, he must carry it with him. Taking the tabernacle key, and preceded by his server, the Priest goes to the Altar.

Genuflecting at the foot of the Altar, the Priest goes up to the Altar and there spreads the corporal; he then opens the tabernacle and once more genuflects, takes out the ciborium and places it upon the corporal. Meanwhile

*the General Confession may be said. The Priest genuflects
and turns to give the Absolution, taking care not to
turn his back to the Blessed Sacrament. The intending
communicants should be kneeling at the Altar Rail.*

THE GENERAL CONFESSION

ALMIGHTY God, Father of our Lord Jesus
Christ, Maker of all things, Judge of all men;
We acknowledge and bewail our manifold sins and
wickedness, Which we, from time to time, most
grievously have committed, By thought, word, and
deed, Against thy Divine Majesty, Provoking most
justly thy wrath and indignation against us. We do
earnestly repent, And are heartily sorry for these
our misdoings; The remembrance of them is grievous
unto us; The burden of them is intolerable. Have
mercy upon us, Have mercy upon us, most merciful
Father; For thy Son our Lord Jesus Christ's sake,
Forgive us all that is past; And grant that we may
ever hereafter Serve and please thee In newness of
life, To the honour and glory of thy Name; Through
Jesus Christ our Lord. Amen.

THE ABSOLUTION

ALMIGHTY God, our heavenly Father, who of
his great mercy hath promised forgiveness of
sins to all those who with hearty repentance and
true faith turn unto him; Have mercy upon you;
pardon ✠ and deliver you from all your sins; confirm and strengthen you in all goodness; and bring
you to everlasting life; through Jesus Christ our
Lord. *Amen.*

Then, turning to the Altar, he genuflects; taking the ciborium in his left hand, he holds a small Host over the open ciborium. He turns to the people and without making the sign of the cross says once:

BEHOLD the Lamb of God: behold him that taketh away the sins of the world.

And then he says thrice:

LORD I am not worthy that thou shouldst come under my roof; but speak the word only and my soul shall be healed.

Afterward the Priest proceeds to communicate the people, beginning at the Epistle side of the sanctuary. In delivering the Sacred Body he says:

THE Body of our Lord Jesus Christ, which was given for thee, preserve thy body and soul unto everlasting life.

When all have communicated, the Priest returns to the Altar, places the ciborium upon the corporal, and genuflects. Then he cleanses his fingers in the vessel of water prepared for that purpose, and wipes them on a purificator; and the water of the ablution is cast into the piscina at a convenient time. He then replaces the ciborium in the tabernacle, genuflects, closes the door of the tabernacle, locks it, and continues:

℣. The Lord be with you.
℟. And with thy spirit.

Let us pray.

ALMIGHTY and everliving God, we most heartily thank thee, for that thou dost vouchsafe to feed us who have duly received these holy mys-

teries, with the spiritual food of the most precious
Body and Blood of thy Son our Saviour Jesus Christ;
and dost assure us thereby of thy favour and goodness
towards us; and that we are very members incorporate in the mystical body of thy Son, which is the
blessed company of all faithful people; and are also
heirs through hope of thy everlasting kingdom, by
the merits of his most precious death and passion.
And we humbly beseech thee, O heavenly Father, so
to assist us with thy grace, that we may continue in
that holy fellowship, and do all such good works
as thou hast prepared for us to walk in; through
Jesus Christ our Lord, to whom, with thee and the
Holy Ghost, be all honour and glory, world without
end. *Amen.*

In Eastertide, the following prayer may be said:

POUR down upon us, O Lord, the Spirit of thy
love: that those whom thou hast satisfied with
the Paschal Sacraments may, of thy goodness, be
made of one heart and of one mind. Through thy
Son Jesus Christ our Lord, who with thee, in the
unity of the same Holy Spirit, liveth and reigneth
God, world without end. *Amen.*

Then he gives the blessing:

THE Peace of God, which passeth all understanding, keep your hearts and minds in the knowledge
and love of God, and of his Son Jesus Christ our
Lord: And the Blessing of God Almighty, the Father,
the ✠ Son, and the Holy Ghost, be amongst you,
and remain with you always. *Amen.*

In some places the following ancient forms of the General Confession and Absolution are in use:

I CONFESS to God Almighty, to blessed Mary ever Virgin, to blessed Michael the Archangel, to blessed John the Baptist, to the holy Apostles Peter and Paul, to all the Saints, and to thee, father, that I have sinned exceedingly in thought, word, and deed: by my fault, by my own fault, by my own most grievous fault. Wherefore I beg blessed Mary ever Virgin, blessed Michael the Archangel, blessed John the Baptist, the holy Apostles Peter and Paul, all the Saints, and thee, father, to pray for me to the Lord our God.

And the Priest says,

ALMIGHTY God have mercy upon you, forgive you your sins, and bring you to everlasting life. *Amen.*

THE Almighty and merciful Lord grant you pardon, ✠ absolution, and remission of your sins. *Amen.*

A NOTE ON RESERVATION

Reservation of the Blessed Sacrament for communicating the sick and those unavoidably absent from the Liturgy is both ancient and ecumenical; but modes of reservation have varied considerably from country to country, and from century to century.

For Anglicans, definite regulations may be found in the Constitutions of Archbishop Peckham, which have been recognized by authority both civil and ecclesiastical as still forming part of the Canon Law of the English Church:

In every parish church there shall be made a *tabernaculum* with a lock, fitting and decent, according to the importance and means of each church, wherein the Body of the Lord Itself shall be placed in a most fair pyx, wrapped in linen, but under no circumstances in a burse, for fear of the Host being crumbled.

The same Constitutions ordered that the Blessed Sacrament be renewed once a week, on Sunday. It is now customary to line the tabernacle with white silk, and to spread a small corporal within it, on which the ciborium or "Most fair pyx" stands. In many places it is customary to veil the ciborium or pyx containing the Blessed Sacrament in white silk, rather than linen. While in use, the tabernacle should be completely covered with a veil of the color of the day. A white or crystal lamp should burn before the tabernacle in which the Blessed Sacrament is reserved.

THE BLESSING OF A CIVIL MARRIAGE

*Adapted from the Scottish Book
of Common Prayer*

*This blessing should be used only if the Priest is
satisfied that the marriage is not contrary to the Canon.
It is fitting that it be given in the Church and before the
Altar.*

*Since this is the blessing of a marriage which has
already taken place, no entry of it should be made in the
Parish Register.*

*The Priest, vested in surplice and white stole, shall
say to the man and the woman,*

FORASMUCH as our Lord hath said, What
God hath joined together, let no man put asunder,
and forasmuch as ye have been joined together in
Holy Matrimony, and have now come hither to ask
the blessing of the Church thereon, I ask you both
whether ye are willing to promise by the help of God
to fulfil the obligations which Christian marriage
demandeth.

Then shall the Priest say to the man,

N. DOST thou promise to love this thy wife, to
comfort her, honour her, and keep her, in
sickness and in health; and forsaking all others, to
keep thee only unto her, so long as ye both shall live?

The man shall answer,

I do.

Then shall the Priest say to the woman,

N. DOST thou promise to love this thy husband,
to comfort him, honour him, and keep him,
in sickness and in health; and, forsaking all others,

to keep thee only unto him, so long as ye both shall live?

The woman shall answer,

I do.

THE BLESSING OF THE RING

Then the ring may be blessed, as follows,

Priest. Our help is in the Name of the Lord.
Answer. Who hath made heaven and earth.

Priest. O Lord, hear my prayer.
Answer. And let my cry come unto thee.

Priest. The Lord be with you.
Answer. And with thy spirit.

Let us pray.

BL✠ESS, O Lord, this Ring, that he who gives it and she who wears it may abide in thy peace, and continue in thy favour, unto their life's end; through Jesus Christ our Lord. *Amen.*

And he may sprinkle the ring with holy water in the form of a cross.

Then the man leaving the ring upon the fourth finger of the woman's left hand, the Priest shall say,

Let us pray.

OUR Father, who art in heaven, Hallowed be thy Name. Thy kingdom come. Thy will be done, On earth as it is in heaven. Give us this day our daily bread. And forgive us our trespasses, As we forgive those who trespass against us. And lead us not into temptation, But deliver us from evil. For thine is the kingdom, and the power, and the glory, for ever and ever. Amen.

Then shall the Priest add,

O ETERNAL God, Creator and Preserver of all mankind, Giver of all spiritual grace, the Author of everlasting life; Send thy blessing upon these thy servants, this man and this woman, whom we bl✠ess in thy Name; that they, living faithfully together, may surely perform and keep the vow and covenant betwixt them made, (whereof this Ring given and received is a token and pledge,) and may ever remain in perfect love and peace together, and live according to thy laws; through Jesus Christ our Lord. *Amen.*

The Priest may add one or both of the following prayers.

O ALMIGHTY God, Creator of mankind, who only art the well-spring of life; Bestow upon these thy servants, if it be thy will, the gift and heritage of children; and grant that they may see their children brought up in thy faith and fear, to the honour and glory of thy Name; through Jesus Christ our Lord. *Amen.*

O GOD, who hast so consecrated the state of Matrimony that in it is represented the spiritual marriage and unity betwixt Christ and his Church; Look mercifully upon these thy servants, that they may love, honour, and cherish each other, and so live together in faithfulness and patience, in wisdom and true godliness, that their home may be a haven of blessing and of peace; through the same Jesus Christ our Lord, who liveth and reigneth with thee and the Holy Spirit ever, one God, world without end. *Amen.*

Then shall the Priest join their hands together, and say,

THOSE whom God hath joined together let no man put asunder.

The man and wife kneeling, the Priest shall add this Blessing.

GOD the Father, God the Son, God the Holy Ghost, bl✠ess, preserve, and keep you; the Lord mercifully with his favour look upon you, and fill you with all spiritual benediction and grace; that ye may so live together in this life, that in the world to come ye may have life everlasting. *Amen.*

And the Priest may sprinkle them with holy water.

The Laying of the Priest's Hand Upon the Sick

Throughout the ages, the Church has used the Laying on of Hands as a special means of grace for the sick. The first of the following forms is from the American Prayer Book; the second is adapted from the Scottish Prayer Book; the third has been adapted from an ancient Western form.

The Priest should wear a violet stole.

Let us pray.

O BLESSED Redeemer, relieve, we beseech thee, by thy indwelling power, the distress of this thy servant; release *him* from sin, and drive away all pain of soul and body, that being restored to soundness of health, *he* may offer thee praise and thanksgiving; who livest and reignest with the Father and the Holy Ghost, one God, world without end. *Amen.*

Then, placing his right hand on the head of the sick person the Priest shall say:

I LAY my hand upon thee, In the Name of the Father, and of the Son, and of the Holy Ghost; beseeching the mercy of our Lord Jesus Christ, that all thy pain and sickness of body being put to flight, the blessing of health may be restored unto thee. Amen.

ANOTHER FORM

***Antiphon.* O Saviour of the world, who by thy Cross and precious Blood hast redeemed us: save us, and help us, we humbly beseech thee, O Lord.**

Psalm 23. *Dominus regit me.*

THE Lord is my shepherd; ★ therefore can I lack nothing.

39

He shall feed me in a green pasture, ★ and lead me forth beside the waters of comfort.

He shall convert my soul, ★ and bring me forth in the paths of righteousness for his Name's sake.

Yea, though I walk through the valley of the shadow of death, I will fear no evil; ★ for thou art with me; thy rod and thy staff comfort me.

Thou shalt prepare a table before me in the presence of them that trouble me; ★ thou hast anointed my head with oil, and my cup shall be full.

Surely thy loving-kindness and mercy shall follow me all the days of my life; ★ and I will dwell in the house of the Lord for ever.

Glory be to the Father, and to the Son, ★ and to the Holy Ghost;

As it was in the beginning, is now, and ever shall be, ★ world without end. Amen.

Antiphon. O Saviour of the world, who by thy Cross and precious Blood hast redeemed us: save us, and help us, we humbly beseech thee, O Lord.

Then, placing his right hand on the head of the sick person, the Priest shall say:

I LAY my hand upon thee, In the Name of the Father, and of the Son, and of the Holy Ghost. Amen.

O ALMIGHTY God, whose blessed Son did lay his hands upon the sick and healed them: Grant we beseech thee, to this person on whom we now lay our hand in his Name, refreshment of spirit and, if it be thy holy will, perfect restoration to health; through the same thy Son Jesus Christ our Lord. *Amen.*

Then shall the Priest say,

THE Almighty Lord, who is a most strong tower to all those who put their trust in him, to whom all things in heaven, in earth, and under the earth, do bow and obey; Be now and evermore thy defence; and make thee know and feel, that there is none other Name under heaven given to man, in whom, and through whom, thou mayest receive health and salvation, but only the Name of our Lord Jesus Christ. *Amen.*

UNTO God's gracious mercy and protection we commit thee. The Lord bl✠ess thee, and keep thee. The Lord make his face to shine upon thee, and be gracious unto thee. The Lord lift up his countenance upon thee, and give thee peace, both now and evermore. *Amen.*

ANOTHER FORM

Let us pray.

ALMIGHTY, everliving God, Maker of mankind, who dost correct those whom thou dost love, and chastise every one whom thou dost receive; We beseech thee to have mercy upon this thy servant visited with thine hand, and to grant that *he* may take *his* sickness patiently, and recover *his* bodily health, if it be thy gracious will; and that, whensoever *his* soul shall depart from the body, it may be without spot presented unto thee; through Jesus Christ our Lord. *Amen.*

At the end of this prayer, the Priest shall lay his right hand upon the head of the sick person, saying:

THEY shall lay hands upon the sick, and they shall recover.

MAY Jesus, the Son of Mary, the Lord and Redeemer of the world, through the merits and intercession of his holy Apostles Peter and Paul, and of all his Saints, show thee favour and mercy. Amen.

Then, blessing the sick person, the Priest shall say:

THE blessing of God Almighty, the Father, the ✠ Son, and the Holy Ghost, descend upon thee and remain with thee always. *Amen.*

Then he may sprinkle the sick person with holy water.

PRAYERS FOR SPECIAL CASES

These may be used as needed, with any of the preceding forms.

For a person mentally disturbed

O HEAVENLY Father, who in thy love and wisdom knowest the anxieties and fears of thy children; whose Son Jesus Christ said to his disciples, It is I, be not afraid; and to the tempest, Peace, be still: Grant that this thy servant may be strengthened to cast all *his* care upon *thee*, for thou carest for *him*. Give *him* quietness; give *him* unshaken trust; and may the day-spring from on high guide *his* feet into the way of peace; through the same Jesus Christ our Lord. *Amen.*

For a person needing sleep

O HEAVENLY Father, who givest thy children sleep for the refreshing of their souls and bodies: Grant this gift to thy servant; keep *him* in that perfect peace which thou hast promised to those whose minds are stayed on thee; inspire *him* with a sense of thy presence; so that in the hours of silence *he* may enjoy the blessed assurance of thy love; through Jesus Christ our Saviour. *Amen.*

For a despondent person

COMFORT, we beseech thee, most gracious God, this thy servant, cast down and faint of heart amidst the sorrows and difficulties of the world; and grant that, by the power of thy Holy Spirit, *he* may be enabled to go upon *his* way rejoicing, and give thee continual thanks for thy sustaining providence; through Jesus Christ our Lord. *Amen.*

For a person troubled in conscience

O BLESSED Lord, the Father of mercies and the God of all comfort: we beseech thee look down in pity and compassion on thy servant whose soul is full of trouble. Give *him* a right understanding of *himself*, and also of thy will for *him*, that he may neither cast away *his* confidence in thee nor place it anywhere but in thee. Deliver *him* from the fear of evil; lift up the light of thy countenance upon *him*, and give *him* thine everlasting peace; through the merits and mediation of Jesus Christ our Lord. *Amen.*

For a person about to undergo an operation

ALMIGHTY God our heavenly Father, we beseech thee graciously to comfort thy servant in *his* suffering, guide the hands of the surgeon, and bless the means made use of for *his* cure. Fill *his* heart with confidence, that though he be sometime afraid, *he* yet may put *his* trust in thee; through Jesus Christ our Lord. *Amen.*

Other suitable prayers will be found on pp. 66–68.

The Blessing of Sick Children

The Priest, wearing a white stole, when he comes to the place where the sick child is, shall say:

℣. Peace be to this house.
℟. And to all that dwell in it.

Then he may sprinkle the sick child, and the bed, and the room, with holy water, saying nothing.

Then he shall say, over the sick child:

Psalm 113. *Laudate, pueri.*

PRAISE the Lord, ye servants; ★ O praise the Name of the Lord.

Blessed be the Name of the Lord ★ from this time forth for evermore.

The Lord's Name is praised ★ from the rising up of the sun unto the going down of the same.

The Lord is high above all nations, ★ and his glory above the heavens.

Who is like unto the Lord our God, that hath his dwelling so high, ★ and yet humbleth himself to behold the things that are in heaven and earth!

He taketh up the simple out of the dust, ★ and lifteth the poor out of the mire;

That he may set him with the princes, ★ even with the princes of his people.

He maketh the barren woman to keep house, ★ and to be a joyful mother of children.

Glory be to the Father, and to the Son, ★ and to the Holy Ghost;

As it was in the beginning, is now, and ever shall be, ★ world without end. Amen.

Lord, have mercy upon us.
Christ, have mercy upon us.
Lord, have mercy upon us.

O UR Father, who art in heaven, Hallowed be thy Name. Thy kingdom come. Thy will be done, On earth as it is in heaven. Give us this day our daily bread. And forgive us our trespasses, As we forgive those who trespass against us. And lead us not into temptation, But deliver us from evil. Amen.

℣. Be merciful, O our God.
℟. Defend the children, O Lord.
℣. Suffer the little children to come unto me.
℟. For of such is the Kingdom of heaven.
℣. O Lord hear my prayer.
℟. And let my cry come unto thee.
℣. The Lord be with you.
℟. And with thy spirit.

Let us pray.

O LORD Jesus Christ, who didst with joy receive and bless the children brought unto thee: Give thy blessing to this thy child; and in thine own time deliver *him* from *his* bodily pain, that *he* may live to serve thee all *his* days. *Amen.*

Let us pray.

O EVERLASTING God, who hast ordained and constituted the services of Angels and men in a wonderful order; Mercifully grant that, as thy holy Angels always do thee service in heaven, so, by thy appointment, they may succour and defend this thy child on earth; through Jesus Christ our Lord. *Amen.*

At the end of this prayer, the Priest shall lay his right hand upon the head of the sick child, saying:

THEY shall lay hands upon the sick, and they shall recover.

MAY Jesus, the Son of Mary, the Lord and Redeemer of the world, through the merits and intercession of his holy Apostles Peter and Paul, and of all his Saints, show thee favour and mercy. Amen.

And blessing the sick child he shall say:

THE blessing of God Almighty, the Father, the ✠ Son, and the Holy Ghost, descend upon thee and remain with thee always. *Amen.*

Then he may sprinkle the sick child with holy water.

NOTE. By ancient custom, children who have not attained the age of reason are not given Holy Unction. The foregoing service may conveniently be used in its place.

The Communion of the Sick with the Reserved Sacrament

When a sick person is to be communicated, the following preparations should be made in his room:

1. A table covered with a clean white cloth, having on it two wax candles (or at least one), which should be lighted during the administration, and a crucifix. Flowers are appropriate.

2. A small glass of fresh water for the ablution after Communion, and a spoon which the Priest may use to administer the ablution to the sick person.

3. A vessel of holy water and a sprinkler.

Traditionally, the Priest who carries the Blessed Sacrament from the Church should be vested in surplice, white stole, and humeral veil; and he should be accompanied by an acolyte or some other devout person, bearing a light and a bell. However this is not always possible at the present day. In any case he should wear a white stole, under his coat if need be. And he should be accompanied, if that be possible.

If the Priest be vested in humeral veil, he will carry the pyx in his hands, covering it with the veil. More usually, he will carry the small pyx in which the Sacrament is taken to the sick in a small burse or pocket of white silk. This should be suspended by a cord passing about the Priest's neck. The burse should be worn under his outer coat or vest, before his breast, and so secured that there will be no danger of dropping or losing the pyx. The Priest should take with him a small corporal and purificator.

It will be found a great convenience if one or two Particles are always kept in the pyx used for sick calls, and the pyx conveniently placed in the tabernacle.

NOTE *that in cases of emergency the Priest may have to administer the Blessed Sacrament to the sick or the dying without the outward tokens of reverence ordinarily displayed. The Priest should at least wear a white stole. The pyx will be kept securely in its burse until the moment of Communion, and should be returned there as soon as Communion has been given.*

On his way to the sick person's house the Priest should recite Psalm 51, and other of the Penitential Psalms. (It is a devout custom that the Priest should be met at the door by some one holding a lighted candle, who should conduct him to the sick person's room.)

As he comes into the sick person's room the Priest should say:

℣. **Peace be to this house.**
℟. **And to all that dwell in it.**

Having spread the corporal on the table prepared, the Priest places the pyx containing the Blessed Sacrament upon it, and genuflects, all present doing likewise. The humeral veil is then laid aside, or the Priest vests in surplice and white stole.

After this, if it be the custom, he may take holy water and sprinkle the sick person, his bed and his room, saying:

Antiphon. **Thou shalt purge me with hyssop, O Lord, and I shall be clean: thou shalt wash me, and I shall be whiter than snow.**

Ps. 51. **Have mercy upon me, O God, after thy great goodness; ⋆ according to the multitude of thy mercies, do away mine offences.**

Glory be to the Father, and to the Son, ⋆ and to the Holy Ghost;

As it was in the beginning, is now, and ever shall be, ★ world without end. Amen.

Antiphon. **Thou shalt purge me with hyssop, O Lord, and I shall be clean: thou shalt wash me, and I shall be whiter than snow.**

℣. Our help is in the Name of the Lord.
℟. Who hath made heaven and earth.
℣. O Lord, hear my prayer.
℟. And let my cry come unto thee.
℣. The Lord be with you.
℟. And with thy spirit.

Let us pray.

GRACIOUSLY hear us, O Lord holy, Father Almighty, everlasting God: and send thy holy Angel from heaven to guard, cherish, protect, visit, and defend all who dwell in this habitation. Through Christ our Lord. *Amen.*

If the sick person desire to confess, the Priest shall hear his confession and absolve him; though in cases where necessity does not urge, the Confession should be made beforehand. If the sick person is to confess the others should leave the sick room until the Priest recalls them after the absolution.

This done, the General Confession shall be said, unless the sick person has just made his confession. But if others are to receive with the sick person, the General Confession and Absolution must be said, even though the sick person has just made his confession. At the time of the distribution of the holy Sacrament, the Priest shall first minister to any who are to communicate with the sick, and last of all to the sick person.

THE GENERAL CONFESSION

ALMIGHTY God, Father of our Lord Jesus Christ, Maker of all things, Judge of all men; We acknowledge and bewail our manifold sins and wickedness, Which we, from time to time, most grievously have committed, By thought, word, and deed, Against thy Divine Majesty, Provoking most justly thy wrath and indignation against us. We do earnestly repent, And are heartily sorry for these our misdoings; The remembrance of them is grievous unto us; The burden of them is intolerable. Have mercy upon us, Have mercy upon us, most merciful Father; For thy Son our Lord Jesus Christ's sake, Forgive us all that is past; And grant that we may ever hereafter Serve and please thee In newness of life, To the honour and glory of thy Name; Through Jesus Christ our Lord. Amen.

Turning toward the sick person, the Priest says

THE ABSOLUTION

ALMIGHTY God, our heavenly Father, who of his great mercy hath promised forgiveness of sins to all those who with hearty repentance and true faith turn unto him; Have mercy upon you; pardon ✠ and deliver you from all your sins; confirm and strengthen you in all goodness; and bring you to everlasting life; through Jesus Christ our Lord. *Amen.*

Then, turning toward the Blessed Sacrament, the Priest may say:

WE do not presume to come to this thy Table, O merciful Lord, trusting in our own righteousness, but in thy manifold and great mercies.

We are not worthy so much as to gather up the crumbs under thy Table. But thou art the same Lord, whose property is always to have mercy: Grant us therefore, gracious Lord, so to eat the flesh of thy dear Son Jesus Christ, and to drink his blood, that our sinful bodies may be made clean by his body, and our souls washed through his most precious blood, and that we may evermore dwell in him, and he in us. *Amen.*

After which the Priest genuflects, takes the pyx, and turning to the sick person, holds the Host in the usual way, so that it be within the rim of the pyx, yet visible. He says once:

BEHOLD the Lamb of God: behold him that taketh away the sins of the world.

Then three times:

LORD, I am not worthy that thou shouldst come under my roof; but speak the word only and my soul shall be healed.

And the Priest gives Holy Communion to the sick person, saying:

THE Body of our Lord Jesus Christ, which was given for thee, preserve thy body and soul unto everlasting life.

If the sick person is dying, it is an ancient custom for the Priest to give Holy Communion using these words in place of the foregoing:

RECEIVE, brother (*or* sister), the Viaticum of the Body of our Lord Jesus Christ; may he deliver thee from the malignant enemy, and bring thee to everlasting life. *Amen.*

Having closed the pyx, the Priest makes the ablution of his fingers, and proceeds:

℣. The Lord be with you.

℟. And with thy spirit.

Let us pray.

A LMIGHTY and everliving God, we most heartily thank thee, for that thou dost vouchsafe to feed us who have duly received these holy mysteries, with the spiritual food of the most precious Body and Blood of thy Son our Saviour Jesus Christ; and dost assure us thereby of thy favour and goodness towards us; and that we are very members incorporate in the mystical body of thy Son, which is the blessed company of all faithful people; and are also heirs through hope of thy everlasting kingdom, by the merits of his most precious death and passion. And we humbly beseech thee, O heavenly Father, so to assist us with thy grace, that we may continue in that holy fellowship, and do all such good works as thou hast prepared for us to walk in; through Jesus Christ our Lord, to whom, with thee and the Holy Ghost, be all honour and glory, world without end. *Amen.*

Or he may say this prayer:

O LORD holy, Father Almighty, everlasting God, we humbly beseech thee that the most holy Body of our Lord Jesus Christ thy Son, which our brother (*or* sister) hath received, may avail for the healing of *his* body and soul. Through the same thy Son Jesus Christ our Lord, who with thee, in the unity of the Holy Spirit, liveth and reigneth God, world without end. *Amen.*

If any particle of the Eucharist remain, the blessing is given in silence by making the sign of the cross with the pyx. If none remain, the blessing is given in the usual way.

THE Peace of God, which passeth all understanding, keep your hearts and minds in the knowledge and love of God, and of his Son Jesus Christ our Lord: And the Blessing of God Almighty, the Father, the ✠ Son, and the Holy Ghost, be amongst you, and remain with you always. *Amen.*

The Priest may give the water of the ablution to the sick person to drink, he may consume it himself, or he may pour it on the ground, or into the fire.

The American Prayer Book provides the following brief form of General Confession and Absolution for optional use at the Communion of the Sick:

THE CONFESSION

O ALMIGHTY Father, Lord of heaven and earth, we confess that we have sinned against thee in thought, word, and deed. Have mercy upon us, O God, after thy great goodness; according to the multitude of thy mercies, do away our offences and cleanse us from our sins; for Jesus Christ's sake. Amen.

THE ABSOLUTION

THE Almighty and merciful Lord grant you ✠ Absolution and Remission of all your sins, true repentance, amendment of life, and the grace and consolation of his Holy Spirit. *Amen.*

NOTE. *If the Blessed Sacrament is to be brought back to the Church, the Priest, as he carries it, recites privately Psalm 148 and other appropriate psalms and hymns.*

When the Priest has arrived at the Church, he places the Sacrament upon the Altar, genuflects and then says:

℣. **Thou gavest them bread from heaven.**
    (*in Eastertide*, **Alleluia** *is added.*)
℞. **Containing in itself all sweetness.**
    (*in Eastertide*, **Alleluia** *is added.*)
℣. **The Lord be with you.**
℞. **And with thy spirit.**

Let us pray.

O GOD, who in a wonderful Sacrament hast left unto us a memorial of thy Passion: grant us, we beseech thee, so to venerate the sacred mysteries of thy Body and Blood, that we may ever perceive within ourselves the fruit of thy redemption. Who livest and reignest, world without end. *Amen.*

Then, in silence, he makes over the people the sign of the cross with the Sacrament in the pyx, and puts it back in the tabernacle.

HOLY UNCTION

Urged by any grave necessity, as in the peril of death, the Priest may anoint the forehead, or one of the organs of sense, with the Oil of the Sick, saying:

BY this holy ✠ Unction, and by his most gracious mercy, the Lord pardon thee whatsoever thou hast done amiss. Amen.

If the sick person survives, the remaining anointings should be supplied, if possible.

NOTE: The form for anointing appointed in the American Prayer Book will be found on page 61; the form appointed in the First Prayer Book on page 62; the ancient Western form on page 63.

SOME GENERAL RUBRICS

Traditionally the Oil of the Sick, sometimes called the Oil of Unction, together with the Oil of the Catechumens and the Holy Chrism, is hallowed by the Bishop of the Diocese at the Eucharist on Maundy Thursday. In case of emergency, the Priest may bless purest olive oil for the anointing of the sick, using the form on page 159.

The Oil of the Sick, together with the other Oils, should be renewed each Eastertide from the supply consecrated on Maundy Thursday. The remainder of the Oils should be reverently burned. The vessels containing the Oils should be carefully kept in a small locked cupboard or aumbry made especially for that purpose. This may be located in the Sanctuary, near the Gospel side of the Altar, or in the sacristy. The keys should always be in the custody of the Priests of the Church. The Oils should never be kept in the tabernacle.

This Sacrament, according to the very ancient use of the Church, should be administered only to those who are gravely ill. But care should be taken that the ad-

ministration be not unduly delayed. In the case of those who are not gravely ill, one of the forms for the laying on of the Priest's hand, pages 39–41, may fittingly be used. The same forms may appropriately be used by the Priest on visits to a sick person subsequent to the administration of Holy Unction.

This Sacrament should not be twice administered during the same illness, unless a partial recovery is followed by a relapse.

Holy Unction may be administered to the unconscious or delirious, if there is no fear of profaning the Sacrament. It ought not to be given to the unbaptized, to the manifestly impenitent, or to the excommunicate.

Children who have not attained the age of reason should not be anointed; the special blessing on page 44 should be given. Nor should those who have never had the use of reason be anointed. But this Sacrament may be administered to those failing through old age.

It is safest to carry the holy Oil absorbed in a piece of cotton, in a small metal box having a screw top, called an Oil Stock. The stock should be carried in a small bag of violet silk.

In the act of anointing the Priest touches the saturated cotton with the tip of his right thumb, and then proceeds to anoint the sick person, making the sign of the cross, and after each anointing, or pair of anointings, a server (if he be in holy Orders), or the Priest himself, wipes the place or places of the anointing with a piece of clean cotton wool. These should afterward be burned by the Priest.

In cases of contagious disease, the Oil may be applied by means of some convenient instrument, e.g., a headless wooden match, with a little cotton wool wrapped around one end; separate instruments may be used for each anointing, all being afterward burned with the cotton used to wipe away the Oil.

In the sick person's room there should be a table covered with a clean white cloth. On it should be placed a crucifix, one or two lighted wax candles, a vessel containing holy water, a dish containing some cotton wool which will be used to remove the holy Oil from the parts anointed, a piece of bread to remove the oil from the Priest's fingers, water to wash his hands and a small towel.

Unless he is certain that he will find all things in readiness, the Priest will do well to bring with him some holy water, a crucifix, a wax candle, and some cotton wool.

If the Sacraments of Penance, the Eucharist, and Unction are to be administered at the same visit, they should be administered in that order, and the introductory prayers of the following office should be shortened or omitted.

If the sick person be unconscious, or physically incapacitated for confessing or communicating, the Priest should absolve the sick person before anointing him, if time allows.

NOTE *that from time to time necessity or charity may demand that this Sacrament be administered without the outward marks of respect set forth above. In any case the Priest should wear a violet stole. He may keep the Oil Stock in its bag until the time of anointing, returning it thereto as soon as the anointing is completed.*

Entering the sick person's room the Priest shall say:

℣. **Peace be to this house.**
℟. **And to all that dwell in it.**

He then places the Oil Stock on the table prepared, and vests in surplice and violet stole. He may sprinkle the sick person, his room, and those present with holy water, saying:

THOU shalt purge me with hyssop, O Lord, and I shall be clean: thou shalt wash me, and I shall be whiter than snow.

If the sick person wishes to make his confession, the Priest will hear it; after which, if time permits, and the sick person be able to bear it, the Priest may briefly instruct the sick person about the Sacrament of Unction. (*See* Saint Mark 6:13 *and* Saint James 5:14–15)

PRELIMINARY PRAYERS WHICH MAY BE SHORTENED OR OMITTED

The Priest then says the following versicles and prayers. These may be shortened or omitted at need.

℣. Our help is in the Name of the Lord.
℟. Who hath made heaven and earth.
℣. The Lord be with you.
℟. And with thy spirit.

Let us pray.

WE beseech thee, O Lord Jesus Christ, that as we thy servants do enter this house, there may also come in everlasting happiness, divine prosperity, unclouded gladness, fruitful charity, eternal health; let no evil spirit approach this place; let the Angels of peace be present, and let all hatred and dissension be done away. Magnify thy holy Name upon us, O Lord, and bl✠ess our conversation; hallow our humble entrance, for thou art holy and gracious, and abidest with the Father and the Holy Spirit, world without end. *Amen.*

LET us pray and beseech our Lord Jesus Christ that in blessing he may bl✠ess this habitation and all who dwell herein, and give his Angel charge concerning them, and make them to serve him, that they may behold the wondrous things of his law. May he turn away from them all hostile powers. May he deliver them from every terror and from all disquietude, and vouchsafe to keep them in health in this dwelling place. Who with the Father and the Holy Spirit, liveth and reigneth God, world without end. *Amen.*

Let us pray.

G RACIOUSLY hear us, O Lord holy, Father Almighty, everlasting God: and send thy holy Angel from heaven to guard, cherish, protect, visit, and defend all who dwell in this habitation. Through Christ our Lord. *Amen.*

Then shall be said the General Confession and Absolution, unless the sick person has just made his confession.

THE GENERAL CONFESSION

A LMIGHTY God, Father of our Lord Jesus Christ, Maker of all things, Judge of all men; We acknowledge and bewail our manifold sins and wickedness, Which we, from time to time, most grievously have committed, By thought, word, and deed, Against thy Divine Majesty, Provoking most justly thy wrath and indignation against us. We do earnestly repent, And are heartily sorry for these our misdoings; The remembrance of them is grievous unto us; The burden of them is intolerable. Have mercy upon us, Have mercy upon us, most merciful Father; For thy Son our Lord Jesus Christ's sake, Forgive us all that is past; And grant that we may ever hereafter Serve and please thee In newness of

life, To the honour and glory of thy Name; Through
Jesus Christ our Lord. Amen.

Turning toward the sick person, the Priest says

THE ABSOLUTION

ALMIGHTY God, our heavenly Father, who of
his great mercy hath promised forgiveness of
sins to all those who with hearty repentance and true
faith turn unto him; Have mercy upon thee; pardon
✠ and deliver thee from all thy sins; confirm and
strengthen thee in all goodness; and bring thee to
everlasting life; through Jesus Christ our Lord.
Amen.

*Before the anointing (the sign of the cross being
made three times over the sick person) the Priest may
say:*

IN the Name of the Fa✠ther, and of the ✠ Son,
and of the Holy ✠ Ghost, may there be ex-
tinguished in thee all power of the devil, by the imposition of our hands, and by the invocation of the
glorious and holy Mother of God, the Virgin Mary,
and of her illustrious spouse Saint Joseph, and of
all the holy Angels, Archangels, Patriarchs, Prophets,
Apostles, Martyrs, Confessors, Virgins, and all the
Saints. *Amen.*

FORMS FOR THE ANOINTING

NOTE. Of the three forms of Unction which follow,
the first is from the American Prayer Book of 1928.
The second, from the First Prayer Book of Edward VI,
has been widely commended for present day use by
Anglican Bishops. The third is the ancient Western
form for administering this Sacrament.

In the actual anointing, the Priest touches the saturated cotton with the tip of his right thumb, and then proceeds to anoint the sick person, making the sign of the Cross as indicated in whichever form of Unction he is using.

Immediately after each anointing, or pair of anointings, a server (if he be in Holy Orders), or the Priest himself, wipes the place or places of the anointing with a piece of clean cotton wool. These should afterward be burned by the Priest.

If the American Form is desired:

O BLESSED Redeemer, relieve, we beseech thee, by thy indwelling power, the distress of this thy servant; release *him* from sin, and drive away all pain of soul and body, that being restored to soundness of health, *he* may offer thee praise and thanksgiving; who livest and reignest with the Father and the Holy Ghost, one God, world without end. *Amen.*

As the Priest anoints the sick person on the forehead he says:

I ANOINT thee with oil, In the Name of the Father, and of the ✠ Son, and of the Holy Ghost; beseeching the mercy of our Lord Jesus Christ, that all thy pain and sickness of body being put to flight, the blessing of health may be restored unto thee. Amen.

If the form from the First Prayer Book is desired:

Then shall the Priest, dipping his thumb in the holy oil, anoint the sick person, in the form of a cross, upon the forehead and breast, saying thus:

A S with this visible oil thy body outwardly is
anointed ✠ : so our heavenly Father, Almighty
God, grant of his infinite goodness that thy soul
inwardly may be anointed ✠ with the Holy Ghost,
who is the Spirit of all strength, comfort, relief, and
gladness. And vouchsafe, for his great mercy, (if it
be his blessed will) to restore unto thee bodily health
and strength, to serve him, and send thee release of
all thy pains, troubles, and diseases, both in body and
in mind. And howsoever his goodness (by his divine
and unsearchable providence) shall dispose of thee;
we, his unworthy ministers and servants, humbly
beseech the eternal Majesty to do with thee according to the multitude of his innumerable mercies, and
to pardon thee all thy sins and offences committed
by all thy bodily senses, passions, and carnal affections; who also vouchsafe mercifully to grant unto
thee ghostly strength, by his Holy Spirit, to with-
stand and overcome all temptations and assaults of
thine adversary, that in no wise he prevail against
thee; but that thou mayest have perfect victory and
triumph against the devil, sin, and death; through
Christ our Lord: who by his death hath overcome the
prince of death; and with the Father and the Holy
Ghost evermore liveth and reigneth God, world
without end. Amen.

Psalm 13. *Usquequo, Domine?*

H OW long wilt thou forget me, O Lord; for
ever? ★ how long wilt thou hide thy face from
me?

How long shall I seek counsel in my soul, and be
so vexed in my heart? ★ how long shall mine enemy
triumph over me?

Consider, and hear me, O Lord my God; ★ lighten mine eyes, that I sleep not in death;

Lest mine enemy say, I have prevailed against him: ★ for if I be cast down, they that trouble me will rejoice at it.

But my trust is in thy mercy, ★ and my heart is joyful in thy salvation.

I will sing of the Lord, because he hath dealt so lovingly with me; ★ yea, I will praise the Name of the Lord Most Highest.

Glory be to the Father, and to the Son, ★ and to the Holy Ghost;

As it was in the beginning, is now, and ever shall be, ★ world without end. Amen.

If the sick person desire to be anointed on the seats of the senses, the Priest may use this ancient Western form:

At the eyes (which should be closed)

By this holy ✠ Unction, and by his most gracious mercy, the Lord pardon thee whatsoever thou hast done amiss by seeing. Amen.

At the ears

By this holy ✠ Unction, and by his most gracious mercy, the Lord pardon thee whatsoever thou hast done amiss by hearing. Amen.

At the nostrils

By this holy ✠ Unction, and by his most gracious mercy, the Lord pardon thee whatsoever thou hast done amiss by smelling. Amen.

At the lips (which should be closed)

By this holy ✠ Unction, and by his most gracious mercy, the Lord pardon thee whatsoever thou hast done amiss by tasting and speaking. Amen.

At the hands (palms of lay persons, backs of hands of priests)

By this holy ✠ Unction, and by his most gracious mercy, the Lord pardon thee whatsoever thou hast done amiss by touching. Amen.

At the feet

By this holy ✠ Unction, and by his most gracious mercy, the Lord pardon thee whatsoever thou hast done amiss by walking. Amen.

The anointing of the feet may be omitted for any reasonable cause.

CONCLUDING PRAYERS

The Priest cleanses his fingers, and continues,

> **Lord, have mercy upon us.**
> ***Christ, have mercy upon us.***
> **Lord, have mercy upon us.**

OUR Father, who art in heaven, Hallowed be thy Name. Thy kingdom come. Thy will be done, On earth as it is in heaven, Give us this day our daily bread. And forgive us our trespasses, As we forgive those who trespass against us. And lead us not into temptation; But deliver us from evil. Amen.

℣. O Lord, save thy servant;
℞. Who putteth *his* trust in thee.
℣. Send *him* help from thy holy place;
℞. And evermore mightily defend *him*.
℣. Let the enemy have no advantage of *him*;
℞. Nor the wicked approach to hurt *him*.
℣. Be unto *him*, O Lord, a strong tower;
℞. From the face of *his* enemy.
℣. O Lord, hear our prayer.
℞. And let our cry come unto thee.
℣. The Lord be with you.
℞. And with thy spirit.

Let us pray.

O LORD God, who by thy holy Apostle James hast said: Is any sick among you? let him call for the Presbyters of the Church; and let them pray over him, anointing him with oil in the Name of the Lord: and the prayer of faith shall save the sick, and the Lord shall raise him up: and if he have committed sins they shall be forgiven him; heal, we beseech thee, O our Redeemer, by the grace of the Holy Spirit, the weakness of this sick person, cure *his* wounds, forgive *his* sins, and cast out from *him* all pain of mind and body, mercifully restore unto *him* soundness both within and without, that made whole by thy gracious aid, *he* may return again to *his* daily course of life. Who with the Father and the same Holy Spirit, livest and reignest God, world without end. *Amen.*

Here may be said any of the Additional Prayers, pages 66, 67 or the Priest may conclude the office with this blessing:

A BLESSING

UNTO God's gracious mercy and protection we commit thee. The Lord bl✠ess thee, and keep thee. The Lord make his face to shine upon thee, and be gracious unto thee. The Lord lift up his countenance upon thee, and give thee peace, both now and evermore. *Amen.*

ADDITIONAL PRAYERS

The first two of the following prayers anciently concluded the administration of Holy Unction:

LOOK down, O Lord, we beseech thee, upon this thy servant *N.*, fainting in weakness of body, and refresh the soul thou hast created; that corrected by thy chastisement, *he* may feel *himself* saved by thy medicine. Through Christ our Lord. *Amen.*

O LORD holy, Father Almighty, everlasting God, who by pouring the grace of thy blessing upon sick bodies, dost preserve, by thy manifold goodness, the work of thy hands: graciously draw near us as we call upon thy Name; deliver thy servant from *his* sickness, and give *him* health; raise *him* up by thy right hand: strengthen *him* by thy might; defend *him* by thy power; and with hope fulfilled restore *him* to thy holy Church. Through Christ our Lord. *Amen.*

O LORD, look down from heaven, behold, visit, and relieve this thy servant. Look upon *him* with the eyes of thy mercy, give *him* comfort and sure confidence in thee, defend *him* in all danger, and keep *him* in perpetual peace and safety; through Jesus Christ our Lord. *Amen.*

O GOD, who knowest us to be set in the midst of so many and great dangers, that by reason of the frailty of our nature we cannot always stand upright: grant to us such strength and protection as may support us in all dangers, and carry us through all temptations; through Jesus Christ our Lord. *Amen.*

When there appeareth but small hope of recovery

O FATHER of mercies, and God of all comfort, our only help in time of need; We fly unto thee for succour in behalf of this thy servant, here lying in great weakness of body. Look graciously upon *him*, O Lord; and the more the outward man decayeth, strengthen *him*, we beseech thee, so much the more continually with thy grace and Holy Spirit in the inner man. Give *him* unfeigned repentance for all the errors of *his* life past, and stedfast faith in thy Son Jesus; that *his* sins may be done away by thy mercy, and *his* pardon sealed in heaven; through the same thy Son, our Lord and Saviour. *Amen.*

VISIT, we beseech thee, O Lord, this thy servant: drive far from *him* all snares of the enemy, let thy holy Angels surround *him* and keep *him* in peace. Through Christ our Lord. *Amen.*

LORD, *he* whom thou lovest is sick; grant *him* all things needful, both for this life and that which is to come. Through Christ our Lord. *Amen.*

For all who are present

O GOD, whose days are without end, and whose mercies cannot be numbered; Make us, we beseech thee, deeply sensible of the shortness and uncertainty of human life; and let thy Holy Spirit lead us in holiness and righteousness, all our days: that, when we shall have served thee in our generation, we may be gathered unto our fathers, having the testimony of a good conscience; in the communion of the Catholic Church; in the confidence of a certain faith; in the comfort of a reasonable, religious, and holy hope; in favour with thee our God, and in perfect charity with the world. All which we ask through Jesus Christ our Lord. *Amen.*

PRAYERS FOR THE DYING

If possible, the Priest should be vested in violet stole. It is a devout custom that a lighted candle burn during the prayers for the dying.

Entering the sick person's room the Priest shall say:

℣. Peace be to this house.
℞. And to all that dwell in it.

Then he may sprinkle the sick person, his room, and the bystanders with holy water, saying:

THOU shalt purge me with hyssop, O Lord, and I shall be clean: thou shalt wash me, and I shall be whiter than snow.

LITANY FOR THE DYING

O GOD the Father;
Have mercy upon the soul of thy servant.
O God the Son;
Have mercy upon the soul of thy servant.
O God the Holy Ghost;
Have mercy upon the soul of thy servant.
O holy Trinity, one God;
Have mercy upon the soul of thy servant.
From all evil, from all sin, from all tribulation;
Good Lord, deliver him.
By thy holy Incarnation, by thy Cross and Passion, by thy precious Death and Burial;
Good Lord, deliver him.
By thy glorious Resurrection and Ascension, and by the coming of the Holy Ghost;
Good Lord, deliver him.
We sinners do beseech thee to hear us, O Lord God; That it may please thee to deliver the soul of

thy servant from the power of the evil one, and from eternal death;

We beseech thee to hear us, good Lord.

That it may please thee mercifully to pardon all *his* sins.

We beseech thee to hear us, good Lord.

That it may please thee to grant *him* a place of refreshment and everlasting blessedness;

We beseech thee to hear us, good Lord.

That it may please thee to give *him* joy and gladness in thy kingdom, with thy saints in light;

We beseech thee to hear us, good Lord.

O Lamb of God, who takest away the sins of the world;

Have mercy upon him.

O Lamb of God, who takest away the sins of the world;

Have mercy upon him.

O Lamb of God, who takest away the sins of the world;

Grant him *thy peace.*

Lord, have mercy.
Christ, have mercy.
Lord, have mercy.

OUR Father, who art in heaven, Hallowed be thy Name. Thy kingdom come. Thy will be done, On earth as it is in heaven. Give us this day our daily bread. And forgive us our trespasses, As we forgive those who trespass against us. And lead us not into temptation, But deliver us from evil. Amen.

Let us pray.

O SOVEREIGN Lord, who desirest not the death of a sinner; We beseech thee to loose the spirit of this thy servant from every bond, and set *him* free from all evil; that *he* may rest with all thy saints in the eternal habitations; through Jesus Christ our Lord, who liveth and reigneth with thee and the Holy Ghost, one God, world without end. *Amen.*

An Absolution to be said by the Priest

THE Almighty and merciful Lord grant thee pardon ✠ and remission of all thy sins, and the grace and comfort of the Holy Spirit. *Amen.*

A Commendation

DEPART, O Christian soul, out of this world, In the Name of God the Father Almighty who created thee.

In the Name of Jesus Christ who redeemed thee.

In the Name of the Holy Ghost who sanctifieth thee.

May thy rest be this day in peace, and thy dwelling place in the Paradise of God.

A Commendatory Prayer when the Soul is Departed

INTO thy hands, O merciful Saviour, we commend the soul of thy servant, now departed from the body. Acknowledge, we humbly beseech thee, a sheep of thine own fold, a lamb of thine own flock, a sinner of thine own redeeming. Reccive *him* into the arms of thy mercy, into the blessed rest of everlasting peace, and into the glorious company of the saints in light. *Amen.*

ADDITIONAL PRAYERS FOR THE DYING

These may be said as needed or desired.

THOU knowest, Lord, the secrets of our hearts; shut not thy merciful ears to our prayer; but spare us, Lord most holy, O God most mighty, O holy and merciful Saviour, thou most worthy Judge eternal, suffer us not, at our last hour, for any pains of death, to fall from thee. *Amen.*

UNTO thee, O Lord, we commend the soul of thy servant *N.*, that dying to the world, *he* may live unto thee: and whatsoever sins *he* hath committed through the frailty of earthly life, we beseech thee to do away by thy most loving and merciful forgiveness; through Jesus Christ our Lord. *Amen.*

O GOD our heavenly Father, in whom we live and move and have our being: Grant to this thy servant grace to desire only thy most holy will; that whether living or dying *he* may be thine; for his sake who loved us and gave himself for us, Jesus Christ our Lord. *Amen.*

O ALMIGHTY God, with whom do live the spirits of just men made perfect after they are delivered from their earthly prisons; We humbly commend the soul of this thy servant, our dear *brother*, into thy hands, as into the hands of a faithful Creator, and most merciful Saviour; beseeching thee, that it may be precious in thy sight. Wash it, we pray thee, in the blood of that immaculate Lamb, that was slain to take away the sins of the world; that whatsoever defilements it may have contracted, through the lusts of the flesh or the wiles of Satan, being purged and done away, it may be presented pure and without spot before thee; through the merits of Jesus Christ thine only Son our Lord. *Amen.*

ALMIGHTY and merciful God, who bestowest upon mankind both the remedies of health and the gifts of life everlasting: look mercifully upon thy servant *N.*, now laboring under great weakness of body, and comfort the soul which thou hast created; so that at the hour of *his* departure, *he* may be presented without spot by the hands of thy holy Angels unto thee, *his* Creator. Through thy Son, Jesus Christ our Lord, who with thee, in the unity of the Holy Spirit, liveth and reigneth God, world without end. *Amen.*

WE beseech thee, Almighty God, mercifully to strengthen this thy servant *N.* by thy grace: that in the hour of death the adversary may not prevail against *him*, but that with thine Angels *he* may enter into life eternal. Through Jesus Christ our Lord. *Amen.*

For a dying child

O LORD Jesus Christ, the only-begotten Son of God, who for our sakes didst become a babe in Bethlehem: We commit unto thy loving care this child whom thou art calling to thyself. Send thy holy angel to lead *him* gently to those heavenly habitations where the souls of those who sleep in thee have perpetual peace and joy, and fold *him* in the everlasting arms of thine unfailing love; who livest and reignest with the Father and the Holy Ghost, one God world without end. *Amen.*

O SAVIOUR of the world, who by thy Cross and precious Blood hast redeemed us; Save us and help us, we humbly beseech thee, O Lord.

At the Reception of the Body

If the body is brought to the Church at a time when the Burial Office is not immediately to follow, this brief office may appropriately be said.

The Priest, vested in surplice, black or purple stole, and cope, meets the body at the entrance of the Church. If it has not already been done, the coffin should here be covered with the Pall, and the Priest may thrice sprinkle the coffin with holy water.

As the procession enters the Church, the following Responsory is begun: it may be said by the Priest or sung by a choir.

COME to *his* assistance, O ye Saints of God: hasten to meet *him*, O ye Angels of the Lord. Receive *his* soul, and offer it in the sight of the Most High.

℣. May Christ, who hath called thee, receive thee, and may the Angels lead thee to Abraham's bosom.

℟. Receive *his* soul, and offer it in the sight of the Most High.

℣. Rest eternal grant unto *him* O Lord: and let light perpetual shine upon *him*.

℟. And offer it in the sight of the Most High.

The coffin should be so placed that, in the case of a lay-person the feet—but if of a priest the head—shall be towards the Altar. According to ancient custom, six, or at least four, lighted candles should stand around the bier.

When the Responsory is ended, the Priest, standing at the entrance of the choir or sanctuary, continues:

Lord, have mercy upon us.
Christ, have mercy upon us.
Lord, have mercy upon us.

74

The Priest says aloud
Our Father, *continuing the prayer in silence.*
Then he says aloud,

℣. And lead us not into temptation.
℟. But deliver us from evil.
℣. From the gate of hell.
℟. Deliver *his* soul O Lord.
℣. May *he* rest in peace.
℟. Amen.
℣. O Lord, hear my prayer.
℟. And let my cry come unto thee.
℣. The Lord be with you.
℟. And with thy spirit.

Let us pray.

ABSOLVE, O Lord, we beseech thee, the soul of thy servant *N.* (thine handmaid *N.*), that, being dead to the world, *he* may live unto thee: and whatsoever *he* hath done amiss in *his* human conversation through frailty of the flesh, do thou wipe away by the pardon of thy merciful goodness. Through Christ our Lord. *Amen.*

Or he may say this prayer:

INTO thy hands, O merciful Saviour, we commend the soul of thy servant, now departed from the body. Acknowledge, we humbly beseech thee, a sheep of thine own fold, a lamb of thine own flock, a sinner of thine own redeeming. Receive *him* into the arms of thy mercy, into the blessed rest of everlasting peace, and into the glorious company of the saints in light. *Amen.*

℣. Rest eternal grant unto *him* O Lord.
℟. And let light perpetual shine upon *him.*
℣. May *he* rest in peace. ℟. Amen.

The Order for
The Burial of the Dead

In several provinces of the Anglican Communion, the use of the following alternative to the Gloria Patri *is authorized:*

Rest eternal grant unto them, O Lord: and let light perpetual shine upon them.

The Priest who officiates at this service is vested in surplice and black or purple stole. In some places it is the custom to wear a cope as well.

¶ *The Minister, meeting the Body, and going before it, either into the Church or towards the Grave, shall say or sing,*

I AM the resurrection and the life, saith the Lord: he that believeth in me, though he were dead, yet shall he live: and whosoever liveth and believeth in me, shall never die.

I know that my redeemer liveth, and that he shall stand at the latter day upon the earth: and though this body be destroyed, yet shall I see God: whom I shall see for myself, and mine eyes shall behold, and not as a stranger.

We brought nothing into this world, and it is certain we can carry nothing out. The Lord gave, and the Lord hath taken away; blessed be the name of the Lord.

¶ *After they are come into the Church, shall be said one or more of the following Selections, taken from the Psalms. The Gloria Patri may be omitted except at the end of the whole portion or selection from the Psalter.*

Dixi, custodiam. Psalm xxxix.

L ORD, let me know mine end, and the number of my days; ★ that I may be certified how long I have to live.

76

Behold, thou hast made my days as it were a span long, and mine age is even as nothing in respect of thee; ★ and verily every man living is altogether vanity.

For man walketh in a vain shadow, and disquieteth himself in vain; ★ he heapeth up riches, and cannot tell who shall gather them.

And now, Lord, what is my hope? ★ truly my hope is even in thee.

Deliver me from all mine offences; ★ and make me not a rebuke unto the foolish.

When thou with rebukes dost chasten man for sin, thou makest his beauty to consume away, like as it were a moth fretting a garment: ★ every man therefore is but vanity.

Hear my prayer, O Lord, and with thine ears consider my calling; ★ hold not thy peace at my tears;

For I am a stranger with thee, and a sojourner, ★ as all my fathers were.

O spare me a little, that I may recover my strength, ★ before I go hence, and be no more seen.

Domine, refugium. Psalm xc.

LORD, thou hast been our refuge, ★ from one generation to another.

Before the mountains were brought forth, or ever the earth and the world were made, ★ thou art God from everlasting, and world without end.

Thou turnest man to destruction; ★ again thou sayest, Come again, ye children of men.

For a thousand years in thy sight are but as yesterday, when it is past, ★ and as a watch in the night.

As soon as thou scatterest them they are even as a sleep; ★ and fade away suddenly like the grass.

In the morning it is green, and groweth up; ★ but in the evening it is cut down, dried up, and withered.

For we consume away in thy displeasure, ★ and are afraid at thy wrathful indignation.

Thou hast set our misdeeds before thee; ★ and our secret sins in the light of thy countenance.

For when thou art angry all our days are gone: ★ we bring our years to an end, as it were a tale that is told.

The days of our age are threescore years and ten; and though men be so strong that they come to fourscore years, ★ yet is their strength then but labour and sorrow; so soon passeth it away, and we are gone.

So teach us to number our days, ★ that we may apply our hearts unto wisdom.

Dominus illuminatio. Psalm xxvii.

THE Lord is my light and my salvation; whom then shall I fear? ★ the Lord is the strength of my life; of whom then shall I be afraid?

One thing have I desired of the Lord, which I will require; ★ even that I may dwell in the house of the Lord all the days of my life, to behold the fair beauty of the Lord, and to visit his temple.

For in the time of trouble he shall hide me in his tabernacle; ★ yea, in the secret place of his dwelling shall he hide me, and set me up upon a rock of stone.

And now shall he lift up mine head ★ above mine enemies round about me.

Therefore will I offer in his dwelling an oblation, with great gladness: ★ I will sing and speak praises unto the Lord.

Hearken unto my voice, O Lord, when I cry unto thee; ★ have mercy upon me, and hear me.

My heart hath talked of thee, Seek ye my face: ★ Thy face, Lord, will I seek.

O hide not thou thy face from me, ★ nor cast thy servant away in displeasure.

Thou hast been my succour; ★ leave me not, neither forsake me, O God of my salvation.

I should utterly have fainted, ★ but that I believe verily to see the goodness of the Lord in the land of the living.

O tarry thou the Lord's leisure; ★ be strong, and he shall comfort thine heart; and put thou thy trust in the Lord.

Deus noster refugium. Psalm xlvi.

GOD is our hope and strength, ★ a very present help in trouble.

Therefore will we not fear, though the earth be moved, ★ and though the hills be carried into the midst of the sea;

Though the waters thereof rage and swell, ★ and though the mountains shake at the tempest of the same.

There is a river, the streams whereof make glad the city of God; ★ the holy place of the tabernacle of the Most Highest.

God is in the midst of her, therefore shall she not be removed; ★ God shall help her, and that right early.

Be still then, and know that I am God: ★ I will be exalted among the nations, and I will be exalted in the earth.

The Lord of hosts is with us; ★ the God of Jacob is our refuge.

Levavi oculos. Psalm cxxi.

I WILL lift up mine eyes unto the hills; ★ from whence cometh my help?

My help cometh even from the Lord, ★ who hath made heaven and earth.

He will not suffer thy foot to be moved; ★ and he that keepeth thee will not sleep.

Behold, he that keepeth Israel ★ shall neither slumber nor sleep.

The Lord himself is thy keeper; ★ the Lord is thy defence upon thy right hand;

So that the sun shall not burn thee by day, ★ neither the moon by night.

The Lord shall preserve thee from all evil; ★ yea, it is even he that shall keep thy soul.

The Lord shall preserve thy going out, and thy coming in, ★ from this time forth for evermore.

De profundis. Psalm cxxx.

OUT of the deep have I called unto thee, O Lord; ★ Lord, hear my voice.

O let thine ears consider well ★ the voice of my complaint.

If thou, Lord, wilt be extreme to mark what is done amiss, ★ O Lord, who may abide it?

For there is mercy with thee; ★ therefore shalt thou be feared.

I look for the Lord; my soul doth wait for him; ★ in his word is my trust.

My soul fleeth unto the Lord before the morning watch; ★ I say, before the morning watch.

O Israel, trust in the Lord, for with the Lord there is mercy, ★ and with him is plenteous redemption.

And he shall redeem Israel ★ from all his sins.

¶ *Then shall follow the Lesson, taken out of the fifteenth Chapter of the first Epistle of St. Paul to the Corinthians.*

1 Corinthians xv. 20.

NOW is Christ risen from the dead, and become the firstfruits of them that slept. For since by man came death, by man came also the resurrection of the dead. For as in Adam all die, even so in Christ shall all be made alive. But every man in his own order: Christ the firstfruits; afterward they that are Christ's at his coming. Then cometh the end, when he shall have delivered up the kingdom to God, even the Father; when he shall have put down all rule and all authority and power. For he must reign, till he hath put all enemies under his feet. The last enemy that shall be destroyed is death. For he hath put all things under his feet. But when he saith all things are put under him, it is manifest that he is excepted, which did put all things under him. And when all things shall be subdued unto him, then shall the Son also himself be subject unto him that put all things under him, that God may be all in all. But some man will say, How are the dead raised up? and with what body do they come? Thou foolish one, that which thou sowest is not quickened, except it die: and that which thou sowest, thou sowest not that body that shall be, but bare grain, it may chance of wheat, or of some other grain: but God giveth it a body as it hath pleased him, and to every seed its own body. All flesh is not the same flesh: but there is one kind of flesh of men, another flesh of beasts, another of fishes, and another of birds. There are also celestial bodies, and bodies terrestrial: but the glory of the celestial is one, and the glory

of the terrestrial is another. There is one glory of
the sun, and another glory of the moon, and another
glory of the stars: for one star differeth from another
star in glory. So also is the resurrection of the dead.
It is sown in corruption; it is raised in incorruption:
it is sown in dishonour; it is raised in glory: it is
sown in weakness; it is raised in power: it is sown
a natural body; it is raised a spiritual body. There
is a natural body, and there is a spiritual body. And
so it is written, The first man Adam was made a
living soul; the last Adam was made a quickening
spirit. Howbeit that was not first which is spiritual,
but that which is natural; and afterward that which
is spiritual. The first man is of the earth, earthy:
the second man is the Lord from heaven. As is the
earthy, such are they also that are earthy: and as
is the heavenly, such are they also that are heavenly.
And as we have borne the image of the earthy, we
shall also bear the image of the heavenly.

Now this I say, brethren, that flesh and blood
cannot inherit the kingdom of God; neither doth
corruption inherit incorruption. Behold, I shew you
a mystery; We shall not all sleep, but we shall all
be changed, in a moment, in the twinkling of an
eye, at the last trump: for the trumpet shall sound,
and the dead shall be raised incorruptible, and we
shall be changed. For this corruptible must put on
incorruption, and this mortal must put on immortality. So when this corruptible shall have put
on incorruption, and this mortal shall have put on
immortality, then shall be brought to pass the saying
that is written, Death is swallowed up in victory.
O death, where is thy sting? O grave, where is thy
victory? The sting of death is sin; and the strength
of sin is the law. But thanks be to God, which giveth

us the victory through our Lord Jesus Christ.
Therefore, my beloved brethren, be ye stedfast, un-
moveable, always abounding in the work of the Lord,
forasmuch as ye know that your labour is not in vain
in the Lord.

¶ *Or this.*

Romans viii. 14.

A S many as are led by the Spirit of God, they
are the sons of God. For ye have not received
the spirit of bondage again to fear; but ye have received the Spirit of adoption, whereby we cry, Abba,
Father. The Spirit himself beareth witness with our
spirit, that we are the children of God: and if children, then heirs; heirs of God, and joint-heirs with
Christ; if so be that we suffer with him, that we may
be also glorified together. For I reckon that the sufferings of this present time are not worthy to be
compared with the glory which shall be revealed in
us. For the earnest expectation of the creature waiteth
for the manifestation of the sons of God. We know
that all things work together for good to them that
love God, to them who are the called according to
his purpose. What shall we then say to these things?
If God be for us, who can be against us? He that
spared not his own Son, but delivered him up for us
all, how shall he not with him also freely give us
all things? Who is he that condemneth? It is Christ
that died, yea rather, that is risen again, who is
even at the right hand of God, who also maketh
intercession for us. Who shall separate us from the
love of Christ? shall tribulation, or distress, or per-
secution, or famine, or nakedness, or peril, or sword?
Nay, in all these things we are more than con-
querors through him that loved us. For I am per-

suaded, that neither death nor life, nor angels, nor principalities, nor powers, nor things present, nor things to come, nor height, nor depth, nor any other creature, shall be able to separate us from the love of God, which is in Christ Jesus our Lord.

¶ *Or this.*

St. John xiv. 1.

JESUS said, Let not your heart be troubled: ye believe in God, believe also in me. In my Father's house are many mansions: if it were not so, I would have told you. I go to prepare a place for you. And if I go and prepare a place for you, I will come again, and receive you unto myself; that where I am, there ye may be also. And whither I go ye know, and the way ye know. Thomas saith unto him, Lord, we know not whither thou goest; and how can we know the way? Jesus saith unto him, I am the way, the truth, and the life: no man cometh unto the Father, but by me.

If a funeral Requiem is to be celebrated, it may be offered at this point.

¶ *Here may be sung a Hymn or Anthem; and, at the discretion of the Minister, the Creed, the Lord's Prayer, the Prayer which followeth, and such other fitting Prayers as are elsewhere provided in this Book, ending with the Blessing; the Minister, before the Prayers, first pronouncing,*

The Lord be with you.
Answer. **And with thy spirit.**
Let us pray.

REMEMBER thy servant, O Lord, according to the favour which thou bearest unto thy people, and grant that, increasing in knowledge and love of thee, *he* may go from strength to strength, in the life of perfect service, in thy heavenly kingdom; through Jesus Christ our Lord, who liveth and reigneth with thee and the Holy Ghost ever, one God, world without end. *Amen.*

UNTO God's gracious mercy and protection we commit you. The Lord bl✠ess you and keep you. The Lord make his face to shine upon you, and be gracious unto you. The Lord lift up his countenance upon you, and give you peace, both now and evermore. *Amen.*

The Apostles' Creed

I BELIEVE in God the Father Almighty, Maker of heaven and earth:

And in Jesus Christ his only Son our Lord: Who was conceived by the Holy Ghost, Born of the Virgin Mary: Suffered under Pontius Pilate, Was crucified, dead, and buried: He descended into hell; The third day he rose again from the dead: He ascended into heaven, And sitteth on the right hand of God the Father Almighty: From thence he shall come to judge the quick and the dead.

I believe in the Holy Ghost: The holy Catholic Church; The Communion of Saints: The Forgiveness of sins: The Resurrection of the body: And the Life ✠ everlasting. Amen.

THE ABSOLUTION OF THE DEAD

Sometimes called The Dismissal of the Body, *this devotion on behalf of the faithful departed is often used after the Funeral Mass. It is occasionally used after other Requiem Masses, especially on All Souls' Day. Also it may be used after the Burial office, if no Requiem is to be said at that time. This service should not be used for a child under seven years of age.*

Music for the Responsory printed below will be found on pages 193 and 194 of The Monastic Diurnal Noted, Volume II.

Words and music of alternative Responsories which may be used in place of the one here given will be found in The Monastic Diurnal Noted, Volume II, *as follows:* Qui Lazarum, *pages* 194, 195; Memento mei, *pages* 198, 199; Libera me . . . de viis, *pages* 206, 207; Libera me . . . de morte, pages 208–210.

If this office follows a Requiem Mass, the Priest remains vested in a black or purple chasuble, or he may wear a cope. He goes to stand at the foot of the bier, where he says the following prayer:

ENTER **not into judgment with thy** *servant*, **O Lord, for in thy sight shall no man living be justified, unless thou grant him remission of all his sins. We therefore beseech thee, let not the sentence of thy judgment press hard upon** *him*, **whom the reasonable prayer of thy faithful Christian people commendeth unto thee: but grant that by the succour of thy grace,** *he* **who while living was sealed with the sign of the Holy Trinity, may be counted worthy to escape thine avenging judgment. Who livest and reignest, world without end.** *Amen.*

This Responsory is then sung or said.

Credo

I KNOW that my Redeemer liveth, and that he shall stand at the latter day upon the earth: and in my flesh shall I see God my Saviour.

℣. Whom I shall see for myself, and mine eye shall behold, and not another.

℟. And in my flesh shall I see God my Saviour.

Toward the end of the Responsory, the Priest puts incense into the censer and blesses it. At the end of the Responsory the Priest says,

> Lord, have mercy upon us.
> *Christ, have mercy upon us.*
> Lord, have mercy upon us.

And the Priest says aloud,

Our Father.

While the Lord's Prayer is being silently repeated, the Priest goes round the bier, sprinkling it with holy water, thrice on each side; and then in like manner he censes it, thrice on each side. Then he says aloud,

℣. And lead us not into temptation.

℟. But deliver us from evil.

℣. From the gate of hell.

℟. Deliver *his* soul O Lord.

℣. May *he* rest in peace.

℟. Amen.

℣. O Lord, hear my prayer.

℟. And let my cry come unto thee.

℣. The Lord be with you.

℟. And with thy spirit.

Let us pray.

The Priest may say the following Collect, or another, chosen from Collects for the Departed (pp. 89–95).

INTO thy hands, O merciful Saviour, we commend the soul of thy servant, now departed from the body. Acknowledge, we humbly beseech thee, a sheep of thine own fold, a lamb of thine own flock, a sinner of thine own redeeming. Receive *him* into the arms of thy mercy, into the blessed rest of ever-lasting peace, and into the glorious company of the Saints in light. Who livest and reignest, world without end. *Amen.*

If the body of the deceased be present, the service ends with the foregoing Collect, or another suitable prayer.

If the body be not present, the Priest, making the sign of the cross over the bier, says,

℣. Rest eternal grant unto *him* O Lord.

℟. And let light perpetual shine upon *him.*

℣. May *he* rest in peace.

℟. Amen.

The first prayer is omitted if the Absolution be made for all the departed.

A complete musical setting of this service may be obtained from The Society of Saint John the Evangelist, Cambridge, Massachusetts, 02138.

While the body is being borne from the Church to the grave, the following anthem may be said or sung:

MAY the Angels lead thee into Paradise; and the Martyrs receive thee at thy coming and bring thee into the holy city Jerusalem. May the choirs of Angels receive thee, and mayest thou, with Lazarus once poor, have everlasting rest.

COLLECTS FOR THE DEPARTED

For all the Faithful Departed

O GOD, the Creator and Redeemer of all the faithful: grant unto the souls of thy servants and handmaids the remission of all their sins; that through devout supplications they may obtain the pardon they have always desired. Who with the Father in the unity of the Holy Spirit, livest and reignest God, world without end. *Amen.*

On the day of Death or Burial

O GOD, whose nature and property is ever to have mercy and to forgive: receive our humble petitions for the soul of thy servant *N.* (thine handmaid *N.*), whom thou hast bidden to depart out of this world: deliver *him* not into the hand of the enemy, neither forget *him* forever; but command thy holy Angels to receive *him* and bring *him* into the country of paradise; that forasmuch as *he* hoped and believed in thee, *he* may possess the joys of eternal life. Through Christ our Lord. *Amen.*

A BSOLVE, O Lord, we beseech thee, the soul of thy servant *N.* (thine handmaid *N.*), that being dead to the world, *he* may live unto thee: and whatsoever *he* hath done amiss in *his* human conversation through frailty of the flesh, do thou wipe away by the pardon of thy merciful goodness. Through Jesus Christ our Lord. *Amen.*

O GOD, whose mercies cannot be numbered; Accept our prayers on behalf of the soul of thy servant departed, and grant *him* an entrance into the land of light and joy, in the fellowship of thy saints; through Jesus Christ our Lord. *Amen.*

REMEMBER thy servant, O Lord, according to the favour which thou bearest unto thy people, and grant that, increasing in knowledge and love of thee, *he* may go from strength to strength, in the life of perfect service, in thy heavenly kingdom; through Jesus Christ our Lord, who liveth and reigneth with thee and the Holy Ghost ever, one God, world without end. *Amen.*

INTO thy hands, O merciful Saviour, we commend the soul of thy servant, now departed from the body. Acknowledge, we humbly beseech thee, a sheep of thine own fold, a lamb of thine own flock, a sinner of thine own redeeming. Receive *him* into the arms of thy mercy, into the blessed rest of everlasting peace, and into the glorious company of the saints in light. *Amen.*

On the third, seventh, and thirtieth days after burial

WE beseech thee, O Lord: that to the soul of thy servant *N.* (thine handmaid *N.*), whose burial three (seven, thirty) days since we now commemorate, thou wouldst vouchsafe to grant the fellowship of thy Saints and elect: and wouldst pour upon *him* the everlasting dew of thy mercy. Through thy Son Jesus Christ our Lord. *Amen.*

On the Anniversary

O GOD, the Lord of mercies: grant unto the soul of thy servant *N.* (thine handmaid *N.*), the anniversary of whose burial we today commemorate, a place of refreshment, the blessedness of repose, and the glory of everlasting light. Through thy Son Jesus Christ our Lord. *Amen.*

ALMIGHTY God, we remember this day before thee thy faithful servant *N.*, and we pray thee that, having opened to *him* the gates of larger life, thou wilt receive *him* more and more into thy joyful service; that *he* may win, with thee and thy servants everywhere, the eternal victory; through Jesus Christ our Lord. *Amen.*

For a departed Bishop

O GOD, who hast made thy servant *N.* to flourish among the Ministers of Apostolic Succession in the honourable office of a Bishop: grant, we beseech thee, that he may also be joined with thine Apostles in a perpetual fellowship. Through thy Son Jesus Christ our Lord. *Amen.*

On the Anniversary of a Bishop

O GOD, the portion in death of those who put their trust in thee: mercifully accept our prayers which we offer on the anniversary of thy servant *N.*, the Bishop; that he who labored faithfully in the service of thy Name, may rejoice in the everlasting company of thy saints. Through thy Son Jesus Christ our Lord. *Amen.*

For a departed Priest

O GOD, who hast made thy servant *N.* to flourish among the Ministers of Apostolic Succession in the honourable office of a Priest: grant, we beseech thee, that he may also be joined with thine Apostles in a perpetual fellowship. Through thy Son Jesus Christ our Lord. *Amen.*

For a Father

O GOD, who hast bidden us to honour our father and mother: of thy mercy have compassion on the soul of *my* father; forgive his sins, and grant that *I* may behold him in the joy of eternal brightness. Through thy Son Jesus Christ our Lord. *Amen.*

For a Mother

O GOD, who hast bidden us to honour our father and mother: of thy mercy have compassion on the soul of *my* mother; forgive her sins, and grant that *I* may behold her in the joy of eternal brightness. Through thy Son Jesus Christ our Lord. *Amen.*

For Parents

O GOD, who hast bidden us to honour our father and mother: of thy mercy have compassion on the souls of *my* father and mother; forgive their sins, and grant that *I* may behold them in the joy of eternal brightness. Through thy Son Jesus Christ our Lord. *Amen.*

For many departed

G RANT, we beseech thee, O Lord, to the souls of thy servants and handmaids thy perpetual mercy: and let it profit them in eternity that they hoped and believed in thee. Through thy Son Jesus Christ our Lord. *Amen.*

O GOD, who declarest thine almighty power most chiefly in showing mercy and pity: receive the supplications and prayers which we offer before thee for the souls of thy servants and handmaidens;

and, forasmuch as in this mortal life they put their trust in thee, vouchsafe them now a place in the glory of thy presence. Through thy Son Jesus Christ our Lord, who with thee in the unity of the Holy Spirit, liveth and reigneth God, world without end. *Amen.*

O GOD, whose nature and property is ever to have mercy and to forgive: have compassion on the souls of thy servants and handmaids, and grant them the remission of all their sins; that being delivered from the bonds of mortality, they may be worthy to pass over into life. Through thy Son Jesus Christ our Lord. *Amen.*

For Brethren

O GOD, the Bestower of pardon, of whom cometh our salvation: we beseech thy mercy for our brethren (*or* sisters) departed out of this present life; that aided by the prayers of blessed Mary ever Virgin, blessed Michael the Archangel, and all the Saints, they may attain to the fellowship of eternal felicity among thine elect; through Jesus Christ our Lord. *Amen.*

For departed members of a Religious Community

O GOD, the Giver of pardon and the Author of man's salvation: we humbly beseech thy mercy to grant that the brethren (*or* sisters) of our Congregation who have departed out of this world, blessed Mary ever Virgin and all thy Saints praying for them, may attain to the fellowship of everlasting blessedness. Through thy Son Jesus Christ our Lord. *Amen.*

For Brethren, Kinsfolk, and Benefactors

O GOD, the Giver of pardon and the Author of man's salvation: we humbly beseech thy mercy to grant that the brethren, (*or* sisters), kinsfolk, and benefactors of our Congregation who have departed out of this world, blessed Mary ever Virgin and all thy Saints praying for them, may attain to the fellowship of everlasting blessedness. Through thy Son Jesus Christ our Lord. *Amen.*

For a Man departed

INCLINE thine ear, O Lord, unto our prayers, wherein we humbly entreat thy mercy: that thou wouldest appoint unto the soul of thy servant *N.*, which thou hast bidden to depart out of this world, a place in the land of life and peace; and wouldest make him a partaker with thy Saints. Through thy Son Jesus Christ our Lord. *Amen.*

For a Woman departed

WE beseech thee, O Lord, of thy loving-kindness have mercy upon the soul of thine handmaid *N.*: and now that she is released from the contagion of mortality, do thou restore her portion in everlasting salvation. Through thy Son Jesus Christ our Lord. *Amen.*

For one who has died suddenly

O ALMIGHTY and merciful God, in whose power is the estate of man: absolve, we beseech thee, the soul of thy servant *N.* (thine handmaid *N.*) from all *his* sins, that although *he* has been overtaken by death, yet *he* may not lose the fruits of repentance which by his will *he* desired. Through thy Son Jesus Christ our Lord. *Amen.*

For those at rest in a Cemetery

O GOD, by whose mercy the souls of the faithful are at rest: favourably grant pardon of their sins to the souls of all thy servants and handmaids, who here and everywhere are at rest in Christ, that being set free from all guilt they may rejoice with thee forever. Through thy Son Jesus Christ our Lord. *Amen.*

For all who have died in the service of our country

ALMIGHTY God, our heavenly Father, in whose hands are the living and the dead; We give thee thanks for all those thy servants who have laid down their lives in the service of our country. Grant to them thy mercy and the light of thy presence, that the good work which thou hast begun in them may be perfected; through Jesus Christ thy Son our Lord. *Amen.*

BLESSING OF A GRAVE IN
UNCONSECRATED GROUND

*Adapted from the Scottish Book
of Common Prayer*

*When the Priest and people have come to the place,
the Priest shall say,*

Let us pray.

O LORD Jesus Christ, who wast laid in the new
tomb of Joseph, and didst thereby sanctify the
grave to be a bed of hope for thy people: Vouchsafe,
we beseech thee, to bless, hal✠low, and consecrate
this grave, that it may be a resting-place, peaceful
and secure, for the body of thy servant which we are
about to commit to thy gracious keeping; who art
the resurrection and the life, and who livest and
reignest with the Father and the Holy Ghost, one
God, world without end. *Amen.*

He may then sprinkle the grave with holy water.

The Burial Service at the Grave

The Priest should be vested in surplice and black or purple stole.

¶ *When they come to the Grave, while the Body is made ready to be laid into the earth, shall be sung or said,*

MAN, that is born of a woman, hath but a short time to live, and is full of misery. He cometh up, and is cut down, like a flower; he fleeth as it were a shadow, and never continueth in one stay.

In the midst of life we are in death; of whom may we seek for succour, but of thee, O Lord, who for our sins art justly displeased?

Yet, O Lord God most holy, O Lord most mighty, O holy and most merciful Saviour, deliver us not into the bitter pains of eternal death.

Thou knowest, Lord, the secrets of our hearts; shut not thy merciful ears to our prayer; but spare us, Lord most holy, O God most mighty, O holy and merciful Saviour, thou most worthy Judge eternal, suffer us not, at our last hour, for any pains of death, to fall from thee.

¶ *Or this.*

ALL that the Father giveth me shall come to me; and him that cometh to me I will in no wise cast out.

He that raised up Jesus from the dead will also quicken our mortal bodies, by his Spirit that dwelleth in us.

Wherefore my heart is glad, and my glory rejoiceth: my flesh also shall rest in hope.

Thou shalt show me the path of life; in thy presence is the fulness of joy, and at thy right hand there is pleasure for evermore.

¶ *Then, while the earth shall be cast upon the Body by some standing by, the Minister shall say,*

UNTO Almighty God we commend the soul of our *brother* departed, and we commit *his* body to the ground; earth to earth, ashes to ashes, dust to dust; in sure and certain hope of the Resurrection unto eternal life, through our Lord Jesus Christ; at whose coming in glorious majesty to judge the world, the earth and the sea shall give up their dead; and the corruptible bodies of those who sleep in him shall be changed, and made like unto his own glorious body; according to the mighty working whereby he is able to subdue all things unto himself.

¶ *Then shall be said or sung,*

I HEARD a voice from heaven, saying unto me, Write, From henceforth blessed are the dead who die in the Lord: even so saith the Spirit; for they rest from their labours.

According to an ancient tradition, this is followed by the Benedictus, *and the repetition of* I heard a voice, *etc.*

Benedictus. St. Luke i. 68.

BLESSED be the Lord God of Israel; ★ for he hath visited and redeemed his people;
  And hath raised up a mighty salvation for us, ★ in the house of his servant David;
  As he spake by the mouth of his holy Prophets, ★ which have been since the world began;
  That we should be saved from our enemies, ★ and from the hand of all that hate us.
  To perform the mercy promised to our forefathers, ★ and to remember his holy covenant;

To perform the oath which he sware to our fore-father Abraham, ★ that he would give us;

That we being delivered out of the hand of our enemies ★ might serve him without fear;

In holiness and righteousness before him, ★ all the days of our life.

And thou, child, shalt be called the prophet of the Highest: ★ for thou shalt go before the face of the Lord to prepare his ways;

To give knowledge of salvation unto his people ★ for the remission of their sins,

Through the tender mercy of our God; ★ whereby the day-spring from on high hath visited us;

To give light to them that sit in darkness, and in the shadow of death, ★ and to guide our feet into the way of peace.

Rest eternal ★ grant unto *him* O Lord.

And let light perpetual ★ shine upon *him.*

I HEARD a voice from heaven, saying unto me, Write, From henceforth blessed are the dead who die in the Lord: even so saith the Spirit; for they rest from their labours.

¶ *Then the Minister shall say,*

The Lord be with you.
Answer. And with thy spirit.

Let us pray.

Lord, have mercy upon us.
Christ, have mercy upon us.
Lord, have mercy upon us.

O UR Father, who art in heaven, Hallowed be thy Name. Thy kingdom come. Thy will be done, On earth as it is in heaven. Give us this day our daily bread. And forgive us our trespasses, As we forgive those who trespass against us. And lead us not into temptation, But deliver us from evil. Amen.

Meanwhile, the Priest may sprinkle the body with holy water.

¶ *Then the Minister shall say one or more of the following Prayers, at his discretion.*

O GOD, whose mercies cannot be numbered; Accept our prayers on behalf of the soul of thy servant departed, and grant *him* an entrance into the land of light and joy, in the fellowship of thy saints; through Jesus Christ our Lord. *Amen.*

A LMIGHTY God, with whom do live the spirits of those who depart hence in the Lord, and with whom the souls of the faithful, after they are delivered from the burden of the flesh, are in joy and felicity; We give thee hearty thanks for the good examples of all those thy servants, who, having finished their course in faith, do now rest from their labours. And we beseech thee, that we, with all those who are departed in the true faith of thy holy Name, may have our perfect consummation and bliss, both in body and soul, in thy eternal and everlasting glory; through Jesus Christ our Lord. *Amen.*

O MERCIFUL God, the Father of our Lord Jesus Christ, who is the Resurrection and the Life; in whom whosoever believeth shall live, though he die; and whosoever liveth, and believeth in him, shall not die eternally; who also hath taught us, by his holy Apostle Saint Paul, not to be sorry, as men without hope, for those who sleep in him; We humbly beseech thee, O Father, to raise us from the death of sin unto the life of righteousness; that, when we shall depart this life, we may rest in him; and that, at the general Resurrection in the last day, we may be found acceptable in thy sight; and receive that blessing, which thy well-beloved Son shall then pronounce to all who love and fear thee, saying, Come, ye blessed children of my Father, receive the kingdom prepared for you from the beginning of the world. Grant this, we beseech thee, O merciful Father, through Jesus Christ, our Mediator and Redeemer. *Amen.*

THE God of peace, who brought again from the dead our Lord Jesus Christ, the great Shepherd of the sheep, through the blood of the everlasting covenant; Make you perfect in every good work to do his will, working in you that which is well pleasing in his sight; through Jesus Christ, to whom be glory for ever and ever. *Amen.*

℣. Rest eternal grant unto *him* O Lord.
℟. And let light perpetual shine upon *him.*
℣. May *he* rest in peace.
℟. Amen.

MAY *his* soul, ✠ and the souls of all the faithful departed, through the mercy of God, rest in peace. *Amen.*

Before departing, the Priest and all others present may once more asperse the grave.

ADDITIONAL COMMITTALS

At the Burial of the Dead at Sea

¶ *The same Office may be used; but instead of the*
Sentence of Committal, the Minister shall say,

UNTO Almighty God we commend the soul of
our *brother* departed, and we commit *his* body
to the deep; in sure and certain hope of the Resurrection unto eternal life, through our Lord Jesus Christ;
at whose coming in glorious majesty to judge the
world, the sea shall give up her dead; and the corruptible bodies of those who sleep in him shall be
changed, and made like unto his glorious body;
according to the mighty working whereby he is
able to subdue all things unto himself.

At a Cremation

UNTO Almighty God we commend the soul of
our *brother* departed, and we commit *his* body
to be consumed by fire; in sure and certain hope of
the Resurrection unto eternal life, through our Lord
Jesus Christ; at whose coming in glorious majesty
to judge the world, the earth and the sea shall give
up their dead; and the corruptible bodies of those
who sleep in him shall be changed, and made like
unto his own glorious body; according to the mighty
working whereby he is able to subdue all things
unto himself.

At the Burial after Cremation

UNTO Almighty God we commend the soul of
our *brother* departed, and we commit *his* ashes
to the ground; earth to earth, dust to dust; in sure
and certain hope of the Resurrection unto eternal
life, through our Lord Jesus Christ; at whose coming

in glorious majesty to judge the world, the earth and the sea shall give up their dead; and the corruptible bodies of those who sleep in him shall be changed, and made like unto his own glorious body; according to the mighty working whereby he is able to subdue all things unto himself.

Or the Minister may say We commit *his* ashes to their resting place.

NOTE that the two preceding committals are adapted from the forms provided by the rubrics of the Scottish Book of Common Prayer.

At the Burial of a Child

According to the ancient custom of the Church, the following service is to be used at the burial of children who die before attaining the age of reason; that is, normally, children under eight years of age.

At the funeral of such children the church bells should be rung joyfully, not tolled as for adults. The Altar may be decorated as for festivals; the vestments should be white. NOTE *that ancient custom forbids a Requiem for baptized infants; if a Mass is desired, a Votive Mass of Saint Michael and all Angels, or of the Holy Guardian Angels may appropriately be offered; or if the funeral take place on an important Holy Day, the Mass of the Day may be offered.*

¶ *The Minister, meeting the Body, and going before it, either into the Church or towards the Grave, shall say,*

I AM the resurrection and the life, saith the Lord: he that believeth in me, though he were dead, yet shall he live: and whosoever liveth and believeth in me, shall never die.

JESUS called them unto him and said, Suffer the little children to come unto me, and forbid them not: for of such is the kingdom of God.

HE shall feed his flock like a shepherd: he shall gather the lambs with his arms, and carry them in his bosom.

¶ *When they are come into the Church, shall be said the following Psalms; and at the end of each Psalm shall be said the Gloria Patri.*

Dominus regit me. Psalm xxiii.

THE Lord is my shepherd; ★ therefore can I lack nothing.

He shall feed me in a green pasture, ★ and lead me forth beside the waters of comfort.

He shall convert my soul, ★ and bring me forth
in the paths of righteousness for his Name's sake.

Yea, though I walk through the valley of the
shadow of death, I will fear no evil; ★ for thou art
with me; thy rod and thy staff comfort me.

Thou shalt prepare a table before me in the
presence of them that trouble me; ★ thou hast
anointed my head with oil, and my cup shall be full.

Surely thy loving-kindness and mercy shall follow
me all the days of my life; ★ and I will dwell in the
house of the Lord for ever.

Glory be to the Father, and to the Son, ★ and to
the Holy Ghost;

As it was in the beginning, is now, and ever shall
be, ★ world without end. Amen.

Levavi oculos. Psalm cxxi.

I WILL lift up mine eyes unto the hills; ★ from
whence cometh my help?

My help cometh even from the Lord, ★ who hath
made heaven and earth.

He will not suffer thy foot to be moved; ★ and he
that keepeth thee will not sleep.

Behold, he that keepeth Israel ★ shall neither
slumber nor sleep.

The Lord himself is thy keeper; ★ the Lord is
thy defence upon thy right hand;

So that the sun shall not burn thee by day, ★
neither the moon by night.

The Lord shall preserve thee from all evil; ★ yea,
it is even he that shall keep thy soul.

The Lord shall preserve thy going out, and thy
coming in, ★ from this time forth for evermore.

Glory be to the Father, and to the Son, ★ and to
the Holy Ghost;

As it was in the beginning, is now, and ever shall be, ★ world without end. Amen.

¶ *Then shall follow the Lesson taken out of the eighteenth Chapter of the Gospel according to St. Matthew.*

AT the same time came the disciples unto Jesus, saying, Who is the greatest in the kingdom of heaven? And Jesus called a little child unto him, and set him in the midst of them, and said, Verily I say unto you, Except ye be converted, and become as little children, ye shall not enter into the kingdom of heaven. Whosoever therefore shall humble himself as this little child, the same is greatest in the kingdom of heaven. And whoso shall receive one such little child in my name receiveth me. Take heed that ye despise not one of these little ones; for I say unto you, That in heaven their angels do always behold the face of my Father which is in heaven.

If the Holy Sacrifice is to be offered, the following Lesson may fittingly be substituted:

St. Mark x. 13

THEY brought young children to Christ, that he should touch them: and his disciples rebuked those that brought them. But when Jesus saw it, he was much displeased, and said unto them, Suffer the little children to come unto me, and forbid them not: for of such is the kingdom of God. Verily I say unto you, Whosoever shall not receive the kingdom of God as a little child, he shall not enter therein. And he took them up in his arms, put his hands upon them, and blessed them.

¶ *Here may be sung a Hymn or an Anthem.*

At this point in the Office, the Holy Sacrifice is offered. After the Mass the Priest changes his chasuble for a white cope; or else he continues the service vested in alb and stole. He goes to stand at the foot of the coffin.

¶ *Then shall the Minister say,*

The Lord be with you.
Answer. **And with thy spirit.**

Let us pray.

Lord, have mercy upon us.
Christ, have mercy upon us.
Lord, have mercy upon us.

¶ *Then shall be said by the Minister and People,*

OUR **Father, who art in heaven, Hallowed be thy Name. Thy kingdom come. Thy will be done, On earth as it is in heaven. Give us this day our daily bread. And forgive us our trespasses, As we forgive those who trespass against us. And lead us not into temptation, But deliver us from evil. Amen.**

While the Lord's Prayer is said, the Priest may thrice sprinkle the coffin with holy water. He does not go round it, nor is it censed.

Minister. **Blessed are the pure in heart;**
Answer. **For they shall see God.**

Minister. **Blessed be the name of the Lord;**
Answer. **Henceforth, world without end.**

Minister. **Lord, hear our prayer;**
Answer. **And let our cry come unto thee.**

¶ *Here shall be said the following Prayers, or other fitting Prayers from this Book.*

O MERCIFUL Father, whose face the angels of thy little ones do always behold in heaven; Grant us stedfastly to believe that this thy child hath been taken into the safe keeping of thine eternal love; through Jesus Christ our Lord. *Amen.*

A LMIGHTY and merciful Father, who dost grant to children an abundant entrance into thy kingdom; Grant us grace so to conform our lives to their innocency and perfect faith, that at length, united with them, we may stand in thy presence in fulness of joy; through Jesus Christ our Lord. *Amen.*

T HE grace of our Lord Jesus ✠ Christ, and the love of God, and the fellowship of the Holy Ghost, be with us all evermore. *Amen.*

While the body is being borne from the Church to the Grave, the following psalm may appropriately be sung or said:

Psalm 148. *Laudate Dominum.*

O PRAISE the Lord from the heavens: ⋆ praise him in the heights.

Praise him, all ye angels of his: ⋆ praise him, all his host.

Praise him, sun and moon: ⋆ praise him, all ye stars and light.

Praise him, all ye heavens, ⋆ and ye waters that are above the heavens.

Let them praise the Name of the Lord: ⋆ for he spake the word, and they were made; he commanded, and they were created.

He hath made them fast for ever and ever: ⋆ he hath given them a law which shall not be broken.

Praise the Lord from the earth, ★ ye dragons and all deeps;

Fire and hail, snow and vapours, ★ wind and storm, fulfilling his word;

Mountains and all hills; ★ fruitful trees and all cedars;

Beasts and all cattle; ★ creeping things and flying fowls;

Kings of the earth, and all peoples; ★ princes, and all judges of the world;

Young men and maidens, old men and children, praise the Name of the Lord: ★ for his Name only is excellent, and his praise above heaven and earth.

He shall exalt the horn of his people: all his saints shall praise him; ★ even the children of Israel, even the people that serveth him.

Glory be to the Father, and to the Son, ★ and to the Holy Ghost;

As it was in the beginning, is now, and ever shall be, ★ world without end. Amen.

FOR THOSE WHO MOURN
FOR A CHILD

O GOD whose ways are hidden, and thy works most wonderful, who makest nothing in vain and lovedst all that thou hast made; Comfort thou thy servants, whose hearts are sore smitten and oppressed; and grant that they may so love and serve thee in this life, that together with this thy child, they may obtain the fulness of thy promises in the world to come; through Jesus Christ our Lord. *Amen.*

—The South African Prayer Book

AT THE GRAVE

¶ *When they are come to the Grave shall be said or sung,*

JESUS saith to his disciples, Ye now therefore have sorrow: but I will see you again, and your heart shall rejoice, and your joy no man taketh from you.

Meanwhile the Priest may sprinkle both the coffin and the grave with holy water, and cense them.

¶ *While the earth is being cast upon the Body, the Minister shall say,*

IN sure and certain hope of the Resurrection to eternal life through our Lord Jesus Christ, we commit the body of this child to the ground. The Lord bless *him* and keep *him*, the Lord make his face to shine upon *him* and be gracious unto *him*, the Lord lift up his countenance upon *him*, and give *him* peace, both now and evermore.

¶ *Then shall be said or sung,*

THEREFORE are they before the throne of God, and serve him day and night in his temple: and he that sitteth on the throne shall dwell among them.

They shall hunger no more, neither thirst any more; neither shall the sun light on them, nor any heat.

For the Lamb which is in the midst of the throne shall feed them, and shall lead them unto living fountains of waters: and God shall wipe away all tears from their eyes.

¶ *Then shall the Minister say,*

The Lord be with you.
Answer. And with thy spirit.

Let us pray.

O GOD, whose most dear Son did take little children into his arms and bless them; Give us grace, we beseech thee, to entrust the soul of this child to thy never-failing care and love, and bring us all to thy heavenly kingdom; through the same thy Son, Jesus Christ our Lord. *Amen.*

ALMIGHTY God, Father of mercies and giver of all comfort; Deal graciously, we pray thee, with all those who mourn, that, casting every care on thee, they may know the consolation of thy love; through Jesus Christ our Lord. *Amen.*

MAY Almighty God, the Father, the ✠ Son, and the Holy Ghost, bless you and keep you, now and for evermore. *Amen.*

Before departing, the Priest and all others present may once more asperse the grave.

The Burial of an Unbaptized Infant

Adapted from the Occasional Offices of the Church of the Province of South Africa.

¶ *On the way to the grave the following sentences may be said,*

HE shall feed his flock like a shepherd: he shall gather the lambs with his arms, and carry them in his bosom.

THE Lord gave, and the Lord hath taken away; blessed be the name of the Lord.

THOU art far from being able to love his creature more than he. For as his majesty is, so also is his mercy.

¶ *When they come to the grave shall be said,*

Psalm 121. *Levavi oculos.*

I WILL lift up mine eyes unto the hills; ★ from whence cometh my help?

My help cometh even from the Lord, ★ who hath made heaven and earth.

He will not suffer thy foot to be moved; ★ and he that keepeth thee will not sleep.

Behold, he that keepeth Israel ★ shall neither slumber nor sleep.

The Lord himself is thy keeper; ★ the Lord is thy defence upon thy right hand;

So that the sun shall not burn thee by day, ★ neither the moon by night.

The Lord shall preserve thee from all evil; ★ yea, it is even he that shall keep thy soul.

The Lord shall preserve thy going out, and thy coming in, ★ from this time forth for evermore.

Glory be to the Father, and to the Son, ★ and to the Holy Ghost;

As it was in the beginning, is now, and ever shall be, ⋆ world without end. Amen.

¶ *Then may be read one of the following:*

St. Matthew xviii. 10.

TAKE heed that ye despise not one of these little ones; for I say unto you, That in heaven their angels do always behold the face of my Father which is in heaven. For the Son of man is come to save that which was lost. How think ye? If a man have an hundred sheep, and one of them be gone astray, doth he not leave the ninety and nine, and goeth into the mountains, and seeketh that which is gone astray? And if so be that he find it, verily I say unto you, he rejoiceth more of that sheep, than of the ninety and nine which went not astray. Even so it is not the will of your Father which is in heaven, that one of these little ones should perish.

Baruch iv. 19.

GO your way, O my children, go your way: for I am left desolate. I have put off the clothing of peace, and put upon me the sack-cloth of my prayer: I will cry unto the Everlasting in my days. Be of good cheer, O my children, cry unto the Lord, and he shall deliver you from the power and hand of the enemies. For my hope is in the Everlasting, that he will save you; and joy is come unto me from the Holy One, because of the mercy which shall soon come unto you from the Everlasting our Saviour. For I sent you out with mourning and weeping: but God will give you to me again with joy and gladness forever.

¶ *As the body is laid in the grave shall be said,*

UNTO God's loving mercy we commit this child, that he may grant *him* a share in the unsearchable riches of the redemption wrought by his Son, our Lord and Saviour Jesus Christ. *Amen.*

¶ *Then shall the Priest say,*

Lord, have mercy upon us.
Christ, have mercy upon us.
Lord, have mercy upon us.

OUR Father, who art in heaven, Hallowed be thy Name. Thy kingdom come. Thy will be done, On earth as it is in heaven. Give us this day our daily bread. And forgive us our trespasses, As we forgive those who trespass against us. And lead us not into temptation, But deliver us from evil. Amen.

Let us pray.

O GOD, whose ways are hidden, and thy works most wonderful, who makest nothing in vain and lovest all that thou hast made; Comfort thou thy servants, whose hearts are sore smitten and oppressed; and grant that they may so love and serve thee in this life, that together with this thy child, they may obtain the fulness of thy promises in the world to come; through Jesus Christ our Lord. *Amen.*

THE grace of our Lord Jesus Christ, and the love of God, and the fellowship of the Holy Ghost, be with us all evermore. *Amen.*

NOTE that this service may be used for the burial of a still-born infant.

THE BURIAL OF PERSONS FOR WHOM THE PRAYER BOOK SERVICE IS NOT APPROPRIATE

See Rubric, page 337 of the Prayer Book

Adapted from the Occasional Offices of the Church of the Province of South Africa.

Psalm 130. *De profundis.*

OUT of the deep have I called unto thee, O
Lord; ★ Lord, hear my voice.

O let thine ear consider well ★ the voice of my complaint.

If thou, Lord, wilt be extreme to mark what is done amiss, ★ O Lord, who may abide it?

For there is mercy with thee; ★ therefore shalt thou be feared.

I look for the Lord; my soul doth wait for him; ★ in his word is my trust.

My soul fleeth unto the Lord before the morning watch; ★ I say, before the morning watch.

O Israel, trust in the Lord; for with the Lord there is mercy, ★ and with him is plenteous redemption.

And he shall redeem Israel ★ from all his sins.

¶ *Then shall follow the Lesson, taken from the Fifth Chapter of St. John's Gospel.*

VERILY, verily, I say unto you, The hour is coming, and now is, when the dead shall hear the voice of the Son of God; and they that hear shall live. For as the Father hath life in himself, so hath he given to the Son to have life in himself; and hath given him authority to execute judgment also, because he is the Son of man. Marvel not at this, for the hour is coming, in the which all that are in the graves shall hear his voice, and shall come forth; they that have done good unto the resurrection of life; and they that have done evil unto the resurrection of judgment. I can of mine own self do nothing; as I hear, I judge: and my judgment is just; because I seek not mine own will, but the will of the Father which hath sent me.

¶ *Then the Minister shall say,*

MAN, that is born of a woman, hath but a short time to live, and is full of misery. He cometh up, and is cut down, like a flower; he fleeth as it were a shadow, and never continueth in one stay.

In the midst of life we are in death; of whom may we seek for succour, but of thee, O Lord, who for our sins art justly displeased?

Yet, O Lord God most holy, O Lord most mighty, O holy and most merciful Saviour, deliver us not into the bitter pains of eternal death.

Thou knowest, Lord, the secrets of our hearts; shut not thy merciful ears to our prayers; but spare us, Lord most holy, O God most mighty, O holy and merciful Saviour, thou most worthy Judge eternal, suffer us not, at our last hour, for any pains of death, to fall from thee.

¶ *After the body is laid in the grave, the Minister shall say,*

WE commit the body of our dear *brother* to the ground; earth to earth, ashes to ashes, dust to dust; and we commend *his* soul to the just and merciful judgment of him who alone hath perfect understanding, even Jesus Christ our Lord.

Let us pray.

Lord, have mercy upon us.
Christ, have mercy upon us.
Lord, have mercy upon us.

OUR Father, who art in heaven, Hallowed be thy Name. Thy kingdom come. Thy will be done, On earth as it is in heaven. Give us this day our daily bread. And forgive us our trespasses, As we forgive those who trespass against us. And lead us not into temptation, But deliver us from evil. Amen.

REMEMBER not, Lord, our offences, nor the offences of our forefathers; neither take thou vengeance of our sins: Spare us, good Lord, spare thy people, whom thou hast redeemed with thy most precious blood, and be not angry with us for ever.

Spare us, good Lord.

ALMIGHTY God, give us grace that we may cast away the works of darkness, and put upon us the armour of light, now in the time of this mortal life, in which thy Son Jesus Christ came to visit us in great humility; that in the last day, when he shall come again in his glorious majesty to judge both the quick and the dead, we may rise to the life immortal, through him who liveth and reigneth with thee and the Holy Ghost, now and ever. *Amen.*

ALMIGHTY God, the fountain of all wisdom, who knowest our necessities before we ask, and our ignorance in asking; We beseech thee to have compassion upon our infirmities; and those things which for our unworthiness we dare not, and for our blindness we cannot ask, vouchsafe to give us, for the worthiness of thy Son Jesus Christ our Lord. *Amen.*

ALMIGHTY God, Father of mercies and giver of all comfort; Deal graciously, we pray thee, with those who mourn, that, casting every care on

thee, they may know the consolation of thy love;
through Jesus Christ our Lord. *Amen.*

O SAVIOUR of the world, who by thy Cross
and precious Blood hast redeemed us; Save
us, and help us, we humbly beseech thee, O Lord.

THE grace of our Lord Jesus Christ, and the
love of God, and the fellowship of the Holy
Ghost, be with us all evermore. *Amen.*

PRAYERS FOR MOURNERS

Collects for the Departed *will be found on pages* 89–95.

For those who mourn a little child

O GOD, whose ways are hidden, and thy works most wonderful, who makest nothing in vain and lovest all that thou hast made; Comfort thou thy servants, whose hearts are sore smitten and oppressed; and grant that they may so love and serve thee in this life, that together with this thy child, they may obtain the fulness of thy promises in the world to come; through Jesus Christ our Lord. *Amen.*

For those in sorrow

O HEAVENLY Father, whose blessed Son Jesus Christ did weep at the grave of Lazarus his friend: Look, we beseech thee, with compassion upon those who are now in sorrow and affliction; comfort them, O Lord, with thy gracious consolations; make them to know that all things work together for good to them that love thee; and grant them evermore sure trust and confidence in thy fatherly care; through the same Jesus Christ our Lord. *Amen.*

ALMIGHTY God, Father of mercies and giver of all comfort; Deal graciously, we pray thee, with those who mourn, that, casting every care on thee, they may know the consolation of thy love; through Jesus Christ our Lord. *Amen.*

ALMIGHTY God, the fountain of all wisdom, who knowest our necessities before we ask, and our ignorance in asking; We beseech thee to have compassion upon our infirmities; and those things which for our unworthiness we dare not, and

119

for our blindness we cannot ask, vouchsafe to give us, for the worthiness of thy Son Jesus Christ our Lord. *Amen.*

For grace to live aright

O HEAVENLY Father, who in thy son Jesus Christ, hast given us a true faith, and a sure hope: help us, we pray thee, to live as those who believe in the Communion of Saints, the forgiveness of sins, and the Resurrection to life everlasting, and strengthen this faith and hope in us all the days of our life, through the love of thy Son, Jesus Christ our Saviour. *Amen.*

For grace to follow the Saints

O GOD the King of Saints, we praise and magnify thy holy Name for all thy servants who have finished their course in thy faith and fear, for the Blessed Virgin Mary, for the holy Patriarchs, Prophets, Apostles, and Martyrs, and for all other thy righteous servants; and we beseech thee that, encouraged by their example, strengthened by their fellowship, and aided by their prayers, we may attain unto everlasting life; through the merits of thy Son Jesus Christ our Lord. *Amen.*

For all who are present

O GOD, whose days are without end, and whose mercies cannot be numbered; Make us, we beseech thee, deeply sensible of the shortness and uncertainty of human life; and let thy Holy Spirit lead us in holiness and righteousness, all our days: that, when we shall have served thee in our genera- tion, we may be gathered unto our fathers, having the testimony of a good conscience; in the communion of the Catholic Church; in the confidence of a certain faith; in the comfort of a reasonable, religious, and holy hope; in favour with thee our God, and in perfect charity with the world. All which we ask through Jesus Christ our Lord. *Amen.*

Part II
BLESSINGS

SOME GENERAL RUBRICS

a. Reserved Blessings

BY ancient Canon Law and the custom of the Church, certain blessings, more usually termed "Consecrations", may be given only by Bishops.

Other blessings, traditionally reserved to Bishops, and Priests especially delegated to give them, are in this book indicated by (R) appearing after the title. These forms include the benediction of those sacred vestments, vessels, and ornaments of the Church, which, according to devout custom, should he hallowed before use.

b. Those who may give Reserved Blessings

THE following, according to the ancient custom of the Church, may give the reserved blessings which are contained in this book:

1. Any Bishop.
2. Parish Priests for their own churches.
3. Other Priests explicitly or implicitly delegated by the Ordinary, within the limits of their jurisdiction, such as Chaplains of schools, hospitals, etc.
4. Superiors of Religious Communities, if Priests, Chaplains—General of Brotherhoods or Sisterhoods, and by delegation Priests or Chaplains of such Communities for their own churches and oratories.

c. Unreserved Blessings

BLESSINGS contained in this book which do not have (R) appearing after the title may traditionally be given by any Priest.

d. Those for whom blessings may be given

BLESSINGS may be given at the request of the faithful, and of those preparing for Baptism; they may also be given at the request of those who are not members of the Church, in order that they may obtain the light of faith, or, together with faith, bodily health.

e. Vesture of the Priest while blessing

IF the Priest performs a blessing immediately before he celebrates Mass, he should ordinarily be vested in Mass vestments without chasuble. At other times he should be vested in surplice and stole of the color of the season (not necessarily of the color of the day) unless the rubrics prescribe a particular color. In giving blessings out of church it may not always be convenient to wear a surplice; but the Priest should not omit to wear a stole.

f. Posture of the Priest while blessing

THE Priest should always give blessings standing, with head uncovered.

g. A caution

GREAT care should be taken that nothing unsuitable is placed on the Altar for blessing. If foodstuffs, etc., are to be blessed in the Church, they should be laid upon a table placed conveniently near the Altar.

h. Forms of blessing

BLESSINGS ought always to be given in the proper form. Every blessing, unless otherwise especially directed, should begin as follows:

℣. *Our help is in the Name of the Lord.*
℟. *Who hath made heaven and earth.*
℣. *The Lord be with you.*
℟. *And with thy spirit.*

Let us pray.

Then is said the prayer or prayers as prescribed; the sign of the cross is made over the object, wherever so indicated. After the prayer or prayers, the object is thrice sprinkled with holy water; to the center, then to the left, lastly to the right.

i. Solemn blessings

IN solemn blessings, all is done as noted in the preceding paragraph, through the prayer or prayers. The Priest then puts incense into the censer three times, saying as he does so, *Be thou blessed by him in whose honour thou art to be burned,* and makes the sign of the cross over the censer. He then sprinkles the object with holy water as noted above, followed by the censing in the same manner.

j. The Server at blessings

IT will be found convenient, particularly in the case of blessings performed at the Altar, to have an acolyte who will minister the holy water (and incense) at the proper time. He may stand at the Priest's right.

THE BLESSING OF WATER

Salt, and pure and clean water, being made ready in the Church or Sacristy, the Priest, vested in surplice and violet stole, shall say,

℣. Our help is in the Name of the Lord.
℟. Who hath made heaven and earth.

And immediately he shall begin the Exorcism of the salt.

I ADJURE thee, O creature of salt, by the living ✠ God, by the true ✠ God, by the holy ✠ God, by God who commanded thee to be cast, by the prophet Elisha, into the water to heal the barrenness thereof, that thou become salt exorcised for the health of believers: and do thou bring to all who take of thee soundness of soul and body, and let all vain imaginations, wickedness, and subtlety of the wiles of the devil, and every unclean spirit fly and depart from every place where thou shalt be sprinkled, adjured by the Name of Him, who shall come to judge both the quick and the dead, and the world by fire. *Amen.*

Let us pray.

ALMIGHTY and everlasting God, we humbly beseech thy great and boundless mercy, that it may please thee of thy loving-kindness to bl✠ess and to hal✠low this creature of salt, which thou hast given for the use of men, let it be to all them that take of it health of mind and body, and let whatsoever shall be touched or sprinkled therewith be free from all uncleanness, and from all assaults of spiritual wickedness. Through Christ our Lord. *Amen.*

Exorcism of the water

I ADJURE thee, O creature of water, by the
Name of God the Father ✠ Almighty, by the
Name of Jesus ✠ Christ his Son our Lord, and by
the power of the Holy ✠ Ghost, that thou become
water exorcised for putting to flight all the power
of the enemy; and do thou avail to cast out and send
hence that same enemy with all his apostate angels:
by the power of the same our Lord Jesus Christ, who
shall come to judge the quick and the dead, and the
world by fire. *Amen.*

Let us pray.

O GOD, who for the salvation of mankind hast
ordained that the substance of water should
be used in one of thy chiefest Sacraments: favourably
regard us who call upon thee, and pour the power
of thy bene✠diction upon this element, made ready
by careful cleansing; that this thy creature, meet
for thy mysteries, may receive the effect of divine
grace, and so cast out devils, and put sickness to
flight, that whatsoever in the dwellings of thy faithful
people shall be sprinkled with this water, may be
free from all uncleanness, and delivered from all
manner of hurt; there let no spirit of pestilence abide,
nor any corrupting air; thence let all the wiles of the
hidden enemy depart, and if there be aught that
layeth snares against the safety or peace of them
that dwell in the house, let it fly before the sprinkling
of this water: so that the health which they seek
through calling upon thy holy Name may be protected against all things that threaten it. Through
Christ our Lord. *Amen.*

*Then the Priest shall cast the salt into the water in
the form of a Cross, saying,*

BE this salt and water mingled together: in the
Name of the Father, and of the ✠ Son, and
of the Holy Ghost. *Amen.*

℣. **The Lord be with you.**
℟. **And with thy spirit.**

Let us pray.

O GOD, who art the Author of unconquered
might, the King of the Empire that cannot be
overthrown, the ever glorious Conqueror: who dost
keep under the strength of the dominion that is
against thee; who rulest the raging of the fierce
enemy; who dost mightily fight against the wickedness of thy foes; with fear and trembling we entreat
thee O Lord, and we beseech thee graciously to
behold this creature of salt and water, mercifully
shine upon it, hallow it with the dew of thy loving-
kindness: that wheresoever it shall be sprinkled,
with the invocation of thy holy Name, all haunting
of the unclean spirit may be driven away; far thence
let the fear of the venomous serpent be cast; and
wheresoever it shall be sprinkled, there let the presence of the Holy Ghost be vouchsafed to all of us
who shall ask for thy mercy. Through Christ our
Lord. *Amen.*

*If water is to be blessed by the celebrant immediately
before the principal Mass on Sunday, he will be wearing
Mass vestments, without the chasuble.*

The Blessing of the Table

This form of Grace at meals, adapted from the ancient office, is widely used on occasions of Retreat. It is in daily use in many Religious Houses.

AT THE MORNING OR MIDDAY MEAL

Before the morning or midday meal, the Priest shall begin,

℣. **Bless ye.**
℟. **Bless ye.**
℣. **The eyes of all**

The rest shall continue,

Wait upon thee, O Lord, and thou givest them their meat in due season; thou openest thine hand, and fillest all things living with plenteousness. Glory be to the Father, and to the Son, and to the Holy Ghost; As it was in the beginning, is now, and ever shall be, world without end. Amen.

Then shall the Priest say,

Let us pray.

BLESS us, O Lord, and these ✠ thy gifts, of which through thy bounty we are about to partake. Through Christ our Lord. *Amen.*

Then the Reader: **Bid, sir, a blessing.**

Priest: **The King of eternal glory make us partakers of his heavenly table.** *Amen.*

At the end of the Lesson from holy Scripture the Reader says,

But thou, O Lord, have mercy upon us.
℟. **Thanks be to God.**

At the end of the meal all shall rise, and the Priest begins,

℣. All thy works praise thee, O Lord.
℟. And thy Saints give thanks unto thee.
℣. Glory be to the Father, and to the Son, and to the Holy Ghost;
℟. As it was in the beginning, is now, and ever shall be, world without end. Amen.

Then shall the Priest say,

WE give thanks to thee, O Almighty God, for all thy benefits. Who livest and reignest, world without end. *Amen.*

AT THE EVENING MEAL

Before the evening meal, the Priest shall begin,

℣. Bless ye.
℟. Bless ye.
℣. The poor shall eat

The rest shall continue,

And be satisfied, they that seek after the Lord shall praise him; your heart shall live forever. Glory be to the Father, and to the Son, and to the Holy Ghost; As it was in the beginning, is now, and ever shall be, world without end. Amen.

Then shall the Priest say,

Let us pray.

BLESS us, O Lord, and these ✠ thy gifts, of which through thy bounty we are about to partake. Through Christ our Lord. *Amen.*

Reader: **Bid, sir, a blessing.**
Priest: **The King of eternal glory bring us to the supper of eternal life.** *Amen.*

At the end of the Lesson from Holy Scripture the Reader says,

But thou, O Lord, have mercy upon us.
Rʒ. **Thanks be to God.**

At the end of the meal all shall rise, and the Priest begins,

Vʒ. **The merciful and gracious Lord hath so done his marvelous works, that they ought to be had in remembrance;**
Rʒ. **He hath given meat unto them that fear him.**
Vʒ. **Glory be to the Father, and to the Son, and to the Holy Ghost;**
Rʒ. **As it was in the beginning, is now, and ever shall be, world without end. Amen.**

Then shall the Priest say,

BLESSED **be the Lord in his gifts, and holy in all his works. Who liveth and reigneth, world without end.** *Amen.*

The Blessing of Gifts and Memorials

The appropriate form of blessing (see Alphabetical Index of Blessings, *page* 284) *should be used.*

After the blessing proper has been performed, one of the appropriate Collects for the Departed, *pages* 89–95, *may be said, if the object be given in memory of one of the faithful departed.*

If a prayer for the donors of the gift or memorial be desired, the following may be added:

O GOD, who by the grace of thy Holy Spirit dost endue the hearts of thy faithful people with the most excellent gift of charity: we beseech thee to keep thy servants, for whom we implore thy mercy, both outwardly in their bodies and inwardly in their souls, that they may love thee with all their hearts and with pure affection perform such things as are acceptable in thy sight. Through Jesus Christ our Lord. *Amen.*

THE BLESSING OF A NEW CROSS

If the Cross is solemnly blessed for use in the Church, this blessing is reserved. But if the blessing is used privately, any Priest may perform it.

The Priest wears a red stole in honour of Christ the King of Martyrs.

℣. Our help is in the Name of the Lord.
℟. Who hath made heaven and earth.
℣. The Lord be with you.
℟. And with thy spirit.

Let us pray.

WE beseech thee, O Lord holy, Father Almighty, everlasting God: that thou wouldst vouchsafe to bl✠ess this sign of the Cross, that it may be a saving remedy for the human race; may it set forward stedfastness in faith, perseverance in good works, and the salvation of souls; may it be a comfort, defence, and shield against all the fiery darts of the enemy. Through Christ our Lord. *Amen.*

Let us pray.

BL✠ESS, O Lord Jesus Christ, this thy Cross, whereby thou didst deliver the world from the power of the devil, and didst by thy Passion overcome the tempter to sin, who rejoiced in the fall of the first man by his eating of the fruit of the forbidden tree. *Here he sprinkles the Cross with holy water.* Be this sign of the Cross hallowed in the Name of the Fa✠ther, and of the ✠Son, and of the Holy✠ Ghost; and may all who shall for the Lord's sake bow down or pray before this Cross, find health of body and soul. Through the same Christ our Lord. *Amen.*

135

Then the Priest genuflects before the Cross, and devoutly venerates and kisses it, and so do any others who may so desire.

Before the Veneration, if the cross is solemnly blessed for use in the Church, the Priest may bless incense, as noted on page 127, and he should thrice cense the cross. And he may wish to add the following prayer:

O GOD, who by the precious Blood of thine only-begotten Son hast vouchsafed to sanctify the Cross to be the sign of our redemption: grant us, we beseech thee, so joyfully to honour that holy Cross, that we may evermore rejoice in thy protection. Through the same Christ our Lord. *Amen.*

NOTE that Crucifixes should be blessed with the form on page 137.

NOTE that small Crosses or Crucifixes, to be borne by the faithful on their persons, may be blessed with the first prayer on page 135. Or the Priest may use this form:

BE thou bl✠essed by him in whose honour thou art to be borne. In the Name of the Father, and of the Son, and of the Holy Ghost. Amen.

THE BLESSING OF
PICTURES AND STATUES

If the picture or statue is to be solemnly blessed for use in the Church, the blessings which follow are reserved. But if the blessings are to be used privately, any Priest may perform them.

A FIGURE OF OUR LORD JESUS CHRIST

℣. Our help is in the Name of the Lord.

℟. Who hath made heaven and earth.

℣. The Lord be with you.

℟. And with thy spirit.

Let us pray.

O LORD Jesus Christ, King of Angels, who art the Way, the Truth, and the Life to those who believe in thee; who for the salvation of the world didst come down from the throne of thy Majesty to earth in great humility, and wast made in the likeness of men: we humbly beseech thee O Lord to bl✠ess, hal✠low, and conse✠crate this figure made in thy honour and memory. Grant that wheresoever it may be placed, the unclean spirit, and all the power of the enemy may straightway depart thence, and by the power of thy benediction let blessing, holiness, and purity there abide. So shall there be giving of thanks unto thee, O Lord God; so shall thy blessing be upon us, and upon all thy people; so shall there descend upon us the plenteousness of thy healthful gifts, O Saviour of the world; who with the Father, in the unity of the Holy Spirit, livest and reignest God, world without end. *Amen.*

A FIGURE OF THE BLESSED VIRGIN MARY

℣. Our help is in the Name of the Lord.

℟. Who hath made heaven and earth.

137

℣. The Lord be with you.

℞. And with thy spirit.

Let us pray.

ALMIGHTY and everlasting God, who hast not forbidden us to carve or paint figures and images of thy Saints, that as often as we look upon their resemblances with our eyes, we may recall their holy examples, and so be stirred up to follow their pattern and holiness: we beseech thee to bl✠ess and hal✠low this figure, fashioned in honour and in memory of the most blessed Virgin Mary, mother of Jesus Christ our Lord and God. Grant that whosoever before this figure shall endeavour worthily to venerate and honour the same most blessed Virgin, may at her intercession obtain grace in this present life, and everlasting glory in that which is to come. Through the same Christ our Lord. *Amen.*

If a shorter form is desired, the Priest may use the following blessing, with appropriate verbal changes.

A FIGURE OF ANY OTHER SAINT

The preceding blessing may be used, with appropriate verbal changes, or the following form may be used:

℣. Our help is in the Name of the Lord.

℞. Who hath made heaven and earth.

℣. The Lord be with you.

℞. And with thy spirit.

Let us pray.

O GOD, the strength of all who put their trust in thee: we beseech thee so to bl✠ess and hal✠low this figure, fashioned in honour of blessed

N. thine (Apostle, *or* Martyr, *or* Bishop, *or* Confessor, *or* Virgin, *etc.*) that all who behold it with devotion may have strength and courage to follow *his* holy example. Through Christ our Lord. *Amen.*

THE BLESSING OF VESTMENTS

The amice, alb, girdle, stole, and chasuble should be blessed before use. The dalmatic, tunicle, cope, and surplice may appropriately be blessed. Cassocks, since they are historically the ordinary garb of the clergy, are not usually classified as vestments.

Vestments which have not been blessed, which the Priest uses in good faith, are not on that account to be considered as blessed.

The sacred vestments lose their blessing if they become so worn, or shapeless, as not to be fit to serve for their particular purpose, or if they have been put to indecent use, or exposed for public sale.

Vestments which have been blessed should not be converted to profane use. If they are burned, the ashes should be thrown into the piscina.

If but one vestment is to be blessed, the prayer following may be said in the singular number.

℣. Our help is in the Name of the Lord.

℟. Who hath made heaven and earth.

℣. The Lord be with you.

℟. And with thy spirit.

Let us pray.

ALMIGHTY and everlasting God, who, by thy servant Moses, didst command vestments to be made for the High Priest, the Priests, and the Levites, that clothed therein, they might perform their office before thee to the honour and glory of thy Name: favorably be near unto us who call upon thee, and vouchsafe to bl✝ess and hal✝low these priestly vestments with thy mighty benediction, by pouring upon them thy grace from above; that so they may become meet and hallowed for divine worship and thy holy mysteries: and grant that

whosoever of thy Bishops, Priests, or Deacons, shall
put them on, may be counted worthy to be saved
and defended against all assaults and temptations;
grant that they may rightly and worthily serve and
frequent thy holy sacraments, and may thereby
persevere in thy service with all godly quietness.
Through Christ our Lord. *Amen.*

THE BLESSING OF STOLES

℣. Our help is in the Name of the Lord.

℟. Who hath made heaven and earth.

℣. The Lord be with you.

℟. And with thy spirit.

Let us pray.

O LORD Jesus Christ, who didst say to thine Apostles, Take my yoke upon you, for my yoke is easy and my burden light: mercifully hear our prayers, and bl✝ess these stoles, that thy servants who shall wear them may so faithfully proclaim thee in Word and Sacrament, that they, and the flocks committed to their care, may obtain thy gift of everlasting life. Who livest and reignest, world without end. *Amen.*

This prayer is based on the words of the Bishop in the Indian Ordinal as he adjusts the stole of the newly ordained Priest, "Take upon thee the yoke of Christ: for his yoke is easy, and his burden light."

THE BLESSING OF A CHURCH ORGAN (R)

℣. Our help is in the Name of the Lord.

℞. Who hath made heaven and earth.

Psalm 150. *Laudate Dominum.*

O PRAISE God in his sanctuary: ★ praise him in the firmament of his power.

Praise him in his noble acts: ★ praise him according to his excellent greatness.

Praise him in the sound of the trumpet: ★ praise him upon the lute and harp.

Praise him in the timbrels and dances: ★ praise him upon the strings and pipe.

Praise him upon the well-tuned cymbals: ★ praise him upon the loud cymbals.

Let every thing that hath breath ★ praise the Lord.

Glory be to the Father, and to the Son, ★ and to the Holy Ghost;

As it was in the beginning, is now, and ever shall be, ★ world without end. Amen.

℣. Praise him in the timbrels and dances.

℞. Praise him upon the strings and pipe.

℣. The Lord be with you.

℞. And with thy spirit.

Let us pray.

O GOD who didst command by thy servant Moses that trumpets should be sounded at the offering of sacrifices in thy Name; and who didst will that the children of Israel should proclaim the glory of thy Name with trumpets also and shawms: bl-✝-ess, we beseech thee, this organ now dedicated to thy worship. Grant that thy faithful people who praise thee on earth with spiritual songs, may be made worthy to attain to eternal joy in heaven.

Through thy Son Jesus Christ our Lord, who with thee, in the unity of the Holy Spirit, liveth and reigneth God, world without end. *Amen.*

If there is a choir, the psalm may appropriately be sung.

THE BLESSING OF THE
STATIONS OF THE CROSS (R)

The Priest should be vested in surplice and violet stole. He should be attended by two acolytes, one of whom ministers the holy water, the other the incense.

After a brief discourse on the value and benefit of the devotion of the Way of the Cross, the Priest shall kneel on the lowest step of the Altar, and the Veni, Creator *shall be sung, all devoutly kneeling.*

Veni, Creator

COME, Holy Ghost, our souls inspire,
And lighten with celestial fire.
Thou the anointing Spirit art,
Who dost thy sevenfold gifts impart.

Thy blessed unction from above,
Is comfort, life, and fire of love,
Enable with perpetual light
The dullness of our blinded sight.

Anoint and cheer our soiled face
With the abundance of thy grace.
Keep far our foes, give peace at home;
Where thou art guide, no ill can come.

Teach us to know the Father, Son,
And thee, of both, to be but One;
That, through the ages all along,
This may be our endless song:

   Praise to thy eternal merit,
   Father, Son, and Holy Spirit. Amen.

℣. O send forth thy Spirit, and they shall be made.
℟. And thou shalt renew the face of the earth.

Let us pray.

O GOD, who didst teach the hearts of thy faithful people, by sending to them the light of thy Holy Spirit: grant us by the same Spirit to have a right judgment in all things, and evermore to rejoice in his holy comfort.

WE beseech thee, O Lord, at the intercession of blessed Mary ever Virgin to defend thy people from all adversity: and to deliver from all assaults of our enemies this thy family which humbly boweth before thee.

DIRECT us, O Lord, in all our doings, with thy most gracious favour, and further us with thy continual help: that in all our works begun, continued, and ended in thee, we may glorify thy holy Name, and finally, by thy mercy, obtain everlasting life. Through thy Son Jesus Christ our Lord, who with thee, in the unity of the Holy Spirit, liveth and reigneth God, world without end. *Amen.*

Then, all standing, the Priest goes to the entrance of the choir or sanctuary, and blesses the Stations. First he blesses the figures or pictures as Images of our Lord, using the form on page 137. Then he sprinkles them with holy water, and censes them. In private chapels the censing may be omitted.

Next he blesses the crosses, which should be made of wood, using the form on page 135. The crosses are sprinkled with holy water as there indicated.

The blessing being finished, the Priest shall proceed to each Station in the usual manner, reading the appropriate meditation and prayers. During the procession, the hymns Vexilla regis *and* Stabat Mater *may be sung, or as much of them as is necessary. When the Priest returns to the sanctuary, the* Te Deum laudamus *shall be sung.*

Te Deum laudamus

WE praise thee, O God, we acknowledge thee to be the Lord.

All the earth doth worship thee, the Father everlasting.

To thee all Angels cry aloud; the Heavens, and all the Powers therein;

To thee Cherubim and Seraphim continually do cry,

Holy, Holy, Holy, Lord God of Sabaoth;

Heaven and earth are full of the Majesty of thy glory.

The glorious company of the Apostles praise thee.

The goodly fellowship of the Prophets praise thee.

The noble army of Martyrs praise thee.

The holy Church throughout all the world doth acknowledge thee;

The Father, of an infinite Majesty;

Thine adorable, true, and only Son;

Also the Holy Ghost, the Comforter.

THOU art the King of Glory, O Christ.

Thou art the everlasting Son of the Father.

When thou tookest upon thee to deliver man, thou didst humble thyself to be born of a Virgin.

When thou hadst overcome the sharpness of death, thou didst open the Kingdom of Heaven to all believers.

Thou sittest at the right hand of God, in the glory of the Father.

We believe that thou shalt come to be our Judge.

The following verse is sung kneeling:

We therefore pray thee, help thy servants, whom thou hast redeemed with thy precious blood.

All rise and continue:

Make them to be numbered with thy Saints, in glory everlasting.

O LORD, save thy people, and bless thine heritage.

Govern them, and lift them up for ever.

Day by day we magnify thee;

And we worship thy Name ever, world without end.

Vouchsafe, O Lord, to keep us this day without sin.

O Lord, have mercy upon us, have mercy upon us.

O Lord, let thy mercy be upon us, as our trust is in thee.

O Lord, in thee have I trusted; let me never be confounded.

℣. We adore thee, O Christ, and we bless thee.

℟. Because by the holy Cross thou hast redeemed the world.

Let us pray.

O GOD, who in the life-giving passion of thy Son hast taught us that only by walking in the way of the Cross may we attain to eternal joys: mercifully grant that as in deep devotion we follow the same thy Son Jesus Christ on the road to Calvary, so we may also share in his everlasting victory. Who with thee, in the unity of the Holy Spirit, liveth and reigneth God, world without end. *Amen.*

Then shall the Priest bless the people present, saying,

THE blessing of God Almighty, the Father, the ✠ Son, and the Holy Ghost, be upon you, and remain with you for ever. *Amen.*

Note that the Stations may be sprinkled and censed collectively from the choir or sanctuary, or individually as the Priest goes to each one; or if more convenient they may be placed in front of the choir or sanctuary step for the blessing and then erected in their places.

THE BLESSING OF A ROOD (R)

The following form of blessing is suggested:

The Priest should be vested in red stole and cope, over the alb or surplice. He should be attended by at least two acolytes, one of whom ministers the holy water, the other the incense.

The Priest and his assistants kneel before the Altar, and the hymn Veni, Creator, *page 145, shall be sung, all devoutly kneeling. Then the Priest stands, and sings the* ℣. *and the collects on page 146.*

All standing, the Priest proceeds to the place where the Rood is set up. And first he blesses the crucifix, using the form on page 137. Then he blesses incense as usual, and censes it thrice.

Next the Priest blesses the figure of the Blessed Virgin Mary, using the form on page 137. The prayer ended, he sprinkles it with holy water thrice, and censes it thrice.

Then he will bless the figure of Saint John, using the form on page 138. The prayer ended, he sprinkles it with holy water thrice, and censes it thrice.

The hymn Te Deum laudamus, *page 147, may then be sung, concluding with the following:*

℣. **We adore thee, O Christ, and we bless thee.**
℞. **Because by thy holy Cross thou hast redeemed the world.**

Let us pray.

ALMIGHTY God, whose most dear Son went not up to joy but first he suffered pain, and entered not into glory before he was crucified: mercifully grant that we, walking in the way of the Cross, may find it none other than the way of life and peace. Through the same thy Son Jesus Christ

150

our Lord, who with thee, in the unity of the Holy
Spirit, liveth and reigneth God, world without end.
Amen.

The Priest may bless the people present, saying,

THE blessing of God Almighty, the Father, the
✠Son, and the Holy Ghost, be upon you and
remain with you for ever. *Amen.*

THE BLESSING OF A PREGNANT WOMAN

This blessing may be given at any time and in any place. The Priest should be vested in surplice and stole of the color of the day.

℣. Our help is in the Name of the Lord.
℞. Who hath made heaven and earth.
℣. O Lord save this woman thy servant;
℞. Who putteth her trust in thee.
℣. Be thou to her a strong tower;
℞. From the face of her enemy.
℣. Send her help from thy holy place.
℞. And evermore mightily defend her.
℣. O Lord hear my prayer.
℞. And let my cry come unto thee.
℣. The Lord be with you.
℞. And with thy spirit.

Let us pray.

ALMIGHTY and everlasting God, who hast given unto thy servants grace, by the confession of a true faith, to acknowledge the glory of the eternal Trinity, and in the power of the Divine Majesty to worship the Unity; We beseech thee that thou wouldest keep thine handmaid *N.*, stedfast in this faith, and evermore defend her from all adversities. Who livest and reignest, one God, world without end. *Amen.*

Let us pray.

O LORD God, Creator of all things, strong and mighty, just yet merciful, who art full of goodness and loving-kindness; who didst deliver Israel from every evil, making our fathers to be thine elect, and hallowing them by thy Spirit; who by the co-operation of the Holy Spirit didst prepare the body

and soul of the glorious Virgin Mary that she might
be made a worthy dwelling place for thy Son; who
didst fill John the Baptist with the Holy Spirit,
causing him to rejoice in his mother's womb: receive
the sacrifice of a contrite heart, and hearken to the
fervent prayer of thine handmaid *N.*, who prayeth
for the preservation of the offspring thou hast given
her to conceive. Continue thy loving-kindness
towards her and defend her from every deceit and
injury of the malignant enemy: that by the protecting
hand of thy mercy, her offspring may happily come
to birth, and, serving thee in its generation in all
things, may at the last be worthy to attain unto
everlasting life. Through the same thy Son Jesus
Christ our Lord, who with thee, in the unity of the
same Holy Spirit, liveth and reigneth God, world
without end. *Amen.*

Here the woman may be sprinkled with holy water.

Psalm 67. *Deus misereatur*

G OD be merciful unto us, and bless us, ★ and
show us the light of his countenance, and be
merciful unto us;

That thy way may be known upon earth, ★ thy
saving health among all nations.

Let the peoples praise thee, O God; ★ yea, let
all the peoples praise thee.

O let the nations rejoice and be glad, ★ for thou
shalt judge the folk righteously, and govern the
nations upon earth.

Let the peoples praise thee, O God; ★ yea, let
all the peoples praise thee.

Then shall the earth bring forth her increase; ★
and God, even our own God, shall give us his blessing.

God shall bless us; ★ and all the ends of the world shall fear him.

Glory be to the Father, and to the Son, ★ and to the Holy Ghost;

As it was in the beginning, is now, and ever shall be, ★ world without end. Amen.

℣. Let us bless the Father, the Son, and the Holy Ghost;

℟. Let us praise him and magnify him forever.

℣. God shall give his Angels charge over thee;

℟. To keep thee in all thy ways.

℣. O Lord hear my prayer.

℟. And let my cry come unto thee.

℣. The Lord be with you.

℟. And with thy spirit.

Let us pray.

VISIT, we beseech thee, O Lord, this habitation, and drive far from it and from thine hand-maiden *N.*, all snares of the enemy: let thy holy Angels dwell herein to preserve her in peace, to-gether with her offspring; and may thy bl✠essing be ever upon her. Save them both, O Lord, and grant unto them thine everlasting light. Through Christ our Lord. *Amen.*

THE blessing of God Almighty, the Father, the ✠Son, and the Holy Ghost, be upon thee and upon thine offspring, and remain with thee always. *Amen.*

THE BLESSING OF CHILDREN

That they may obtain the mercy of God

In some places it is customary, on the feast of the Holy Innocents, or on some other day, for the young children of the parish to be brought to the Church for a special blessing. The following form will be found appropriate.

This same blessing may appropriately be given to one or more children at any time, at the request of parents or guardians.

The Priest who gives this blessing should be vested in surplice and white stole.

℣. **Our help is in the Name of the Lord.**
℟. **Who hath made heaven and earth.**
℣. **The Lord be with you.**
℟. **And with thy spirit.**

Let us pray.

O LORD Jesus Christ, Son of the Living God, who didst say, Suffer the little children to come unto me, for of such is the kingdom of heaven: favourably regard the faith and devotion of these parents; pour the fulness of thy bl✠essing upon *these children;* that increasing in wisdom and stature, and in favour with God and man, they may reach a blessed old age, and at length obtain the reward of eternal life. Who livest and reignest, world without end. *Amen.*

Then may be said or sung:

Psalm 113. *Laudate, pueri.*

PRAISE the Lord, ye servants; ★ O praise the Name of the Lord.
Blessed be the Name of the Lord ★ from this time forth for evermore.

The Lord's Name is praised ★ from the rising up of the sun unto the going down of the same.

The Lord is high above all nations, ★ and his glory above the heavens.

Who is like unto the Lord our God, that hath his dwelling so high, ★ and yet humbleth himself to behold the things that are in heaven and earth!

He taketh up the simple out of the dust, ★ and lifteth the poor out of the mire;

That he may set him with the princes, ★ even with the princes of his people.

He maketh the barren woman to keep house, ★ and to be a joyful mother of children.

Glory be to the Father, and to the Son, ★ and to the Holy Ghost;

As it was in the beginning, is now, and ever shall be, ★ world without end. Amen.

Then shall the Priest say,

> Lord, have mercy upon us.
> *Christ, have mercy upon us.*
> Lord, have mercy upon us.

Then shall be said by the Priest and people,

OUR Father, who art in heaven, Hallowed be thy Name. Thy kingdom come. Thy will be done, On earth as it is in heaven. Give us this day our daily bread. And forgive us our trespasses, As we forgive those who trespass against us. And lead us not into temptation, But deliver us from evil. Amen.

And the Priest shall bless the child or children, saying,

THE blessing of God Almighty, the Father, the ✠ Son, and the Holy Ghost, descend upon you and remain with you always. *Amen.*

THE BLESSING OF THROATS

Traditionally, this blessing for health is given on February 3, the feast of Saint Blasius, Bishop and Martyr. However, it may be given as desired at any time during the year, and in any place.

The blessing is given to the faithful with two candles blessed according to the following form:

THE BLESSING OF THE TWO CANDLES

℣. Our help is in the Name of the Lord.
℟. Who hath made heaven and earth.
℣. O Lord, hear my prayer.
℟. And let my cry come unto thee.
℣. The Lord be with you.
℟. And with thy spirit.

Let us pray.

ALMIGHTY and most merciful God, who hast created all things by the power of thy Word, and who, for the salvation of man, hast willed that that same Word, by whom all things were made should become incarnate; thou who art great and doest wondrous things, awesome and worthy of praise: for the confession of whose faith the glorious Martyr and Bishop Blasius, spurning divers torments, was counted worthy to receive the martyr's palm: to whom, among other gifts thou didst grant the virtue of healing infirmities of the throat through thine almighty power; we humbly beseech thy majesty that, regarding not our sins, thou wouldst deign to bl✝ess, through his prayers and merits, this creature of wax, sanctifying and hallowing it through thy grace: that all who with a lively faith receive its impress upon their throats, may be freed from all ailments of the same, and being restored to

157

health, may show forth in thy holy Church their thankfulness for thy benefits, by praising thy glorious Name, which is worthy of eternal benediction, through Jesus Christ our Lord. *Amen.*

The candles may then be sprinkled with holy water.

THE BLESSING OF THROATS

If this blessing is given immediately after Mass, the Priest will be vested in alb and stole of the color of the Mass; at other times he should be vested in surplice and red stole.

Placing the two candles in the form of a cross, the Priest applies them to the throats of those who desire the blessing (who should be kneeling at the Altar Rail), saying:

THROUGH the intercession of blessed Blasius, may God free thee from all affections of the throat, and from all other ailments: In the Name of the Father, and of the ✠ Son, and of the Holy Ghost. *Amen.*

NOTE. Saint Blasius, the martyred Bishop of Sebaste in Armenia, was also a skilful physician. Tradition tells us that on his way to martyrdom he healed a child who was choking to death of an obstruction in his throat. While the blessing which bears his name is given to the throat in memory of his charitable act, it is to be thought of not only as a blessing of the throat, but also as a blessing for bodily health in general.

THE BLESSING OF OIL

This blessing, anciently appointed for the Oil of Unction, should be used by a Priest only in emergencies when the Oil of the Sick blessed by the Bishop cannot be obtained.

The oil to be blessed should be the purest olive oil obtainable. The Priest should be vested in surplice and violet stole.

℣. Our help is in the Name of the Lord.
℟. Who hath made heaven and earth.

The Exorcism

I ADJURE thee, O creature of oil, by God the Father ✠ Almighty, who made heaven and earth, the sea and all that therein is. Let all the power of the adversary, all the host of the devil, and all haunting and vain imaginations of Satan be cast out, and flee away from this creature of oil; that it may be to all who shall use it health of mind and body, in the Name of God the Father ✠ Almighty, and of Jesus ✠ Christ his Son our Lord, and of the Holy ✠ Spirit the Comforter, for the love of the same our Lord Jesus Christ, who shall come to judge the quick and the dead, and the world by fire. *Amen.*

℣. O Lord hear my prayer.
℟. And let my cry come unto thee.
℣. The Lord be with you.
℟. And with thy spirit.

Let us pray.

O LORD God Almighty, whom all the hosts of Angels do serve with fear and trembling, and who dost accept their spiritual service, vouchsafe to behold, to bl✠ess, and to hal✠low this creature of oil, which thou hast brought forth from the sap

159

of the olive tree, and with which thou hast commanded
the sick to be anointed, that they may receive health,
and give thanks unto thee the living and true God:
grant, we beseech thee; that all who shall be anointed
with this oil which we bl✠ess in thy Name, may be
set free from all weakness, from all sickness, and
from all the craft of the enemy, and let every hostile
power be kept away from the work of thine hands,
which thou hast redeemed with the precious blood
of thy Son, Jesus Christ our Lord. Who with thee,
in the unity of the Holy Spirit, liveth and reigneth
God, world without end. *Amen.*

The Blessing of Salt to be Used in Baptism

"And then he" that is, the Priest, "puts hallowed salt into his mouth" that is, the mouth of the child whom he is baptizing, "to signify the spiritual salt, which is the Word of God, wherewith he should be seasoned."

—*Ceremonies to be used in the Church of England,* an explanation set forth by authority in 1543.

Where this ancient custom, traditionally known as the Imposition of Salt, *has been restored, the salt to be used for this purpose should first be blessed according to the following formula:*

I ADJURE thee, O creature of salt, in the Name of God the Father ✠ Almighty, in the charity of our Lord Jesus ✠ Christ, and in the power of the Holy ✠ Spirit. I adjure thee by the living ✠ God, by the true ✠ God, the holy ✠ God, by God ✠ who created thee for the protection of the human race, and who commanded thee to be hallowed by his servants for the use of those coming to belief, that in the Name of the Holy Trinity thou mayest be effective as an healthful agent for putting the enemy to flight. Wherefore we pray thee, O Lord our God, that in sanctifying this creature of salt thou wouldst sanc✠tify it; and in blessing it thou wouldst bl✠ess it, that it may become to all who receive it a perfect remedy abiding within them, in the Name of the same our Lord Jesus Christ, who shall come to judge the quick and the dead, and the world by fire. *Amen.*

The salt should be white, pulverized, clean, and dry. Once blessed, the salt may be used on the occasion of subsequent baptisms. It should not be used for any other purpose.

The manner of administering the salt is as follows. Immediately after the prayer Almighty and immortal God, the aid of all who believe *in the Order for Holy Baptism, the Priest takes a few grains of the hallowed salt between his right thumb and index finger, and placing the salt in the mouth of the person to be baptized, says,*

RECEIVE the salt of wisdom: may it be unto thee a pledge of everlasting life. *Amen.*

The salt may be blessed during the Baptismal Office, immediately before it is to be administered, or the Priest may bless it privately in the sacristy.

BENEDICTION OF CROSSES
FOR THE PLANTING

*Set forth by the Convocation of the Philippine
Episcopal Church*

*At the time of planting, and preferably on some day
of rest traditionally observed by the people, may be said
the following office.*

*Before the service, crosses of wood, or of reeds, or of
some other suitable material, shall be placed in a convenient manner close to the Epistle corner of the Altar.*

*The Priest, vested in a purple Cope, shall enter,
accompanied by attendants and, standing before the
middle of the Altar, shall begin,*

℣. **Our help is in the Name of the Lord.**
℟. **Who hath made heaven and earth.**
℣. **O God, make speed to save us.**
℟. **O Lord, make haste to help us.**

Our Father.

*Then shall he recite with the people the following
Psalm.*

Psalm 65. *Te decet hymnus.*

**THOU, O God, art praised in Sion; ★ and unto
thee shall the vow be performed in Jerusalem.**
**Thou that hearest the prayer, ★ unto thee shall all
flesh come.**
**My misdeeds prevail against me; ★ O be thou
merciful unto our sins.**
**Blessed is the man whom thou choosest, and
receivest unto thee: ★ he shall dwell in thy court,
and shall be satisfied with the pleasures of thy
house, even of thy holy temple.**

Thou shalt show us wonderful things in thy righteousness, O God of our salvation; ★ thou that art the hope of all the ends of the earth, and of them that remain in the broad sea.

Who in his strength setteth fast the mountains, ★ and is girded about with power.

Who stilleth the raging of the sea, ★ and the noise of his waves, and the madness of the peoples.

They also that dwell in the uttermost parts of the earth shall be afraid at thy tokens, ★ thou that makest the out-goings of the morning and evening to praise thee.

Thou visitest the earth, and blessest it; ★ thou makest it very plenteous.

The river of God is full of water: ★ thou preparest their corn, for so thou providest for the earth.

Thou waterest her furrows; thou sendest rain into the little valleys thereof; ★ thou makest it soft with drops of rain, and blessest the increase of it.

Thou crownest the year with thy goodness; ★ and thy clouds drop fatness.

They shall drop upon the dwellings of the wilderness; ★ and the little hills shall rejoice on every side.

The folds shall be full of sheep; ★ the valleys also shall stand so thick with corn, that they shall laugh and sing.

Glory be to the Father, and to the Son, ★ and to the Holy Ghost;

As it was in the beginning, is now, and ever shall be, ★ world without end. Amen.

At the conclusion of the Psalm he shall proceed to the Epistle corner of the Altar and, facing the people, shall read the Lesson.

The Lesson. Isaiah lxv. 17

F OR, behold, I create new heavens and a new earth: and the former shall not be remembered, nor come into mind. But be ye glad and rejoice forever in that which I create: for, behold, I create Jerusalem a rejoicing and her people a joy. And I will rejoice in Jerusalem, and joy in my people: and the voice of weeping shall be no more heard in her, nor the voice of crying. There shall be no more thence an infant of days, nor an old man that hath not filled his days: for the child shall die an hundred years old; but the sinner being an hundred years old shall be accursed. And they shall build houses, and inhabit them; and they shall plant vineyards, and eat the fruit of them. They shall not build, and another inhabit; they shall not plant, and another eat: for as the days of a tree are the days of my people, and mine elect shall long enjoy the work of their hands. They shall not labour in vain, nor bring forth for trouble; for they are the seed of the blessed of the Lord, and their offspring with them. And it shall come to pass, that before they call, I will answer; and while they are yet speaking, I will hear. The wolf and the lamb shall feed together, and the lion shall eat straw like the bullock: and dust shall be the serpent's meat. They shall not hurt nor destroy in all my holy mountain, saith the Lord.

At the conclusion of the Lesson, he shall begin,

℣. The eyes of all wait upon thee, O Lord;

℟. And thou givest them their meat in due season.

℣. Thou openest thine hand,

℟. And fillest all things living with plenteousness.

℣. The Lord be with you.

℟. And with thy spirit.

Let us pray.

O GOD, by the promise of whose beloved Son we are assured that we shall not want such things as we need: bless these crosses we have brought to thine Altar, and grant that in the fields where we place them they may stand in sign of our unfailing trust in thy bounty, and as encouragement to all who mark their witness to put their faith in thy providence and conform their lives to the true growth of thy Holy Spirit. Through the same thy Son Jesus Christ our Lord, who with thee, in the unity of the same Holy Spirit, liveth and reigneth God, world without end. *Amen.*

Then the Priest may asperse and cense the crosses.

Immediately afterward shall be sung a Mass of the Rogation; or the Litany may first be sung in Procession around the bounds of some adjoining field, the Procession then returning to the Church for the Mass.

If the Litany be sung in this manner, the Priest shall set up one of the crosses at the boundary of the field, first saying,

℣. The Lord be with you.
℟. And with thy spirit.

SET up thy cross, O Lord, as an ensign to the people, and draw all nations unto it.

Then he may asperse and cense this cross.

It is advised that no private field may be chosen for this Rogation Procession, but some field or garden appertaining to the Mission, and that the Priest take occasion, either before the Procession or in a Sermon during the Mass, to explain to the people that what is done in this particular field is done on behalf of all.

After the Mass the people shall take the crosses and place them in their fields, there to remain until the harvest.

Offering of the First Fruits

*Set forth by the Convocation of the Philippine
Episcopal Church*

*At the time of harvest, and preferably on some day of
rest traditionally observed by the people, shall be sung
the Mass appointed for Thanksgiving Day.*

*After the Kyrie, the Priest, standing at the Epistle
corner of the Altar, shall say,*

Let us pray.

GRANT us, O God, to remember always the
abundance of thy goodness to us, and as stewards of thy bounty to make due return from the
harvest of our lives. Through thy Son Jesus Christ
our Lord, who with thee, in the unity of the Holy
Spirit, liveth and reigneth God, world without end.
Amen.

Then shall be read the Lesson.

The Lesson. Deuteronomy xxvi. 1

AND it shall be, when thou art come in unto the
land which the Lord thy God giveth thee for
an inheritance, and possessest it, and dwellest therein;
that thou shalt take of the first of all the fruit of the
earth, which thou shalt bring of thy land that the
Lord thy God giveth thee, and shalt put it in a
basket, and shalt go unto the place which the Lord
thy God shall choose to put his Name there. And
thou shalt go unto the priest that shall be in those
days, and say unto him, I profess this day unto the
Lord thy God, that I am come unto the country
which the Lord sware unto our fathers for to give us.
And the priest shall take the basket out of thine
hand, and set it down before the altar of the Lord
thy God. And thou shalt speak and say before the

Lord thy God, A Syrian ready to perish was my
father, and he went down into Egypt, and sojourned
there with a few, and became there a nation, great,
mighty, and populous. And the Egyptians evil
entreated us, and afflicted us, and laid upon us hard
bondage. And when we cried unto the Lord God of
our fathers, the Lord heard our voice, and looked
on our affliction, and our labour and our oppression.
And the Lord brought us forth out of Egypt with a
mighty hand, and with an outstretched arm, and
with great terribleness, and with signs and with
wonders; and he hath brought us into this place, and
hath given us this land, even a land that floweth with
milk and honey. And now, behold, I have brought
the first fruits of the land, which thou, O Lord, hast
given me. And thou shalt set it before the Lord thy
God, and worship before the Lord thy God. And
thou shalt rejoice in every good thing which the
Lord thy God hath given unto thee, and unto thine
house, thou, and the levite, and the stranger that is
among you.

At the conclusion of the Lesson shall be said,

Alleluia. ℣. *Ps.* 67. Let the peoples praise thee,
O God; let all the peoples praise thee. ℣. Then shall
the earth bring forth her increase; and God, even
our own God, shall give us his blessing.

*Then shall follow the Collect, Epistle, Gospel, and
Creed.*

*At the Offertory the people shall place in a convenient
receptacle before the Altar bundles of grain representing
the first-fruits of their harvest. These the Priest shall
cense, after placing them on or near the Epistle corner
of the Altar. Then he shall say,*

℣. The Lord be with you.

℟. And with thy spirit.

Let us pray.

O GOD, Creator and sustainer of mankind, receive, we beseech thee, these first-fruits of our harvest, and help us in all our deeds, and in the hopes that move them, to offer to thee our first and our best. Through thy Son, Jesus Christ our Lord. *Amen.*

NOTE *that a brief form for blessing of the First Fruits will be found on page* 200.

THE BLESSING OF A NEW HOUSE

*In some places the devout custom is followed of having
the Priest who solemnizes a marriage bless the dwelling
of the newly married couple, using the form provided
below. The same office may fittingly be used for blessing
any dwelling at the request of the faithful.*

A brief form of blessing will be found on page 198.

*The Priest should be vested in surplice and stole of
the color of the season. Standing in the Oratory or chief
room of the house, he shall say,*

DEARLY beloved brethren, let us pray our Lord
God favorably to shine upon this dwelling, to
fill this house with godly inhabitants, and ever to
defend them with the protection of his divine Majesty.

℣. Our help is in the Name of the Lord.
℞. Who hath made heaven and earth.
℣. The Lord be with you.
℞. And with thy spirit.

Let us pray.

WE humbly beseech thee, O God the Father
Almighty, on behalf of this house, of all who
dwell here, and of all things therein: that it may
please thee to bl✠ess and hal✠low this house, and
to fill it with all good; grant, O Lord, unto all who
dwell here abundance of heavenly blessing to sustain
their life, and so direct the desires of their hearts
that they may effectually obtain thy mercy. Therefore at our coming in, may it please thee to bl✠ess
and to hal✠low this house, even as thou wert pleased
to bless the house of Abraham, Isaac, and Jacob,
and may Angels of light dwell within the walls of
this house, to keep all the inhabitants thereof in
peace. Through Christ our Lord. *Amen.*

*Then the Priest shall sprinkle the room with holy
water, and afterwards shall go through all the rooms of
the house, sprinkling each with holy water in the form of
a cross.*

In the meantime shall be said or sung,

Antiphon. **Thou shalt purge me with hyssop, O
Lord, and I shall be clean: thou shalt wash me, and
I shall be whiter than snow.**

Psalm 51. *Miserere mei, Deus.*

HAVE mercy upon me, O God, after thy great
goodness; ★ according to the multitude of thy
mercies do away mine offences.

Wash me throughly from my wickedness, ★ and
cleanse me from my sin.

For I acknowledge my faults, ★ and my sin is
ever before me.

Against thee only have I sinned, and done this
evil in thy sight; ★ that thou mightest be justified in
thy saying, and clear when thou shalt judge.

Behold, I was shapen in wickedness, ★ and in sin
hath my mother conceived me.

But lo, thou requirest truth in the inward parts,
★ and shalt make me to understand wisdom secretly.

Thou shalt purge me with hyssop, and I shall be
clean; ★ thou shalt wash me, and I shall be whiter
than snow.

Thou shalt make me hear of joy and gladness, ★
that the bones which thou hast broken may rejoice.

Turn thy face from my sins, ★ and put out all my
misdeeds.

Make me a clean heart, O God, ★ and renew a
right spirit within me.

Cast me not away from thy presence, ★ and take not thy holy Spirit from me.

O give me the comfort of thy help again, ★ and stablish me with thy free Spirit.

Then shall I teach thy ways unto the wicked, ★ and sinners shall be converted unto thee.

Deliver me from blood-guiltiness, O God, thou that are the God of my health; ★ and my tongue shall sing of thy righteousness.

Thou shalt open my lips, O Lord, ★ and my mouth shall show thy praise.

For thou desirest no sacrifice, else would I give it thee; ★ but thou delightest not in burnt-offerings.

The sacrifice of God is a troubled spirit: ★ a broken and contrite heart, O God, shalt thou not despise.

O be favourable and gracious unto Sion; ★ build thou the walls of Jerusalem.

Then shalt thou be pleased with the sacrifice of righteousness, with the burnt-offerings and oblations; ★ then shall they offer young bullocks upon thine altar.

Glory be to the Father, and to the Son, ★ and to the Holy Ghost;

As it was in the beginning, is now, and ever shall be, ★ world without end. Amen.

If more psalms are needed, any of the following may be used:

Psalm 46, p. 244; Psalm 65 p. 163; Psalms 15, 26, 28, 29, 48, 76, 84, 87, 112, 119 (part one).

Antiphon. Thou shalt purge me with hyssop, O Lord, and I shall be clean: thou shalt wash me, and I shall be whiter than snow.

When the whole house has been sprinkled, the Priest shall return to the Oratory or chief room and shall say,

℣. The Lord be with you.
℟. And with thy spirit.

Let us pray.

GRACIOUSLY hear us, O Lord holy, Father Almighty, everlasting God: and send thy holy Angel from heaven to guard, cherish, protect, visit, and defend all who dwell in this habitation. Through Christ our Lord. *Amen.*

LET this house be hallowed; let every unclean spirit fly hence, by the power of our Lord Jesus Christ: may health, joy, and cheerfulness be given to all who dwell herein, and may thy Majesty ever protect and preserve them, O Almighty God, who livest and reignest, throughout all ages, world without end. *Amen.*

THE blessing of God Almighty, the Father, the ✠ Son, and the Holy Ghost, be upon this house and all who dwell herein, now and forevermore. *Amen.*

The Blessing of Houses
on the Feast of the Epiphany

It is an Eastern custom for the Parish Priest to bless the dwellings of his parishioners on the feast of the Epiphany. In places where the faithful desire such a blessing, the following form, which derives from Eastern sources, may appropriately be used.

The Priest should be vested in surplice and white stole. Standing in the Oratory or chief room of the house, he shall begin the service by saying,

℣. **Peace be to this house.**
℟. **And to all that dwell in it.**

Then shall be sung or said,

Antiphon. **From the east there came wise men to Bethlehem, to worship the Lord; and when they had opened their treasures, they presented unto him precious gifts: gold as to a mighty King, incense as to the true God, and myrrh to foreshew his burial, alleluia.**

Magnificat. St. Luke i. 46.

MY soul doth magnify the Lord, ⋆ and my spirit hath rejoiced in God my Saviour.

For he hath regarded ⋆ the lowliness of his handmaiden.

For behold, from henceforth ⋆ all generations shall call me blessed.

For he that is mighty hath magnified me; ⋆ and holy is his Name.

And his mercy is on them that fear him ⋆ throughout all generations.

He hath showed strength with his arm; ⋆ he hath scattered the proud in the imagination of their hearts.

He hath put down the mighty from their seat, ★ and hath exalted the humble and meek.

He hath filled the hungry with good things; ★ and the rich he hath sent empty away.

He remembering his mercy hath holpen his servant Israel; ★ as he promised to our forefathers, Abraham and his seed, for ever.

Glory be to the Father, and to the Son, ★ and to the Holy Ghost;

As it was in the beginning, is now, and ever shall be, ★ world without end. Amen.

Meanwhile he may sprinkle the place with holy water, and also cense it. Then the antiphon is repeated:

From the east there came wise men to Bethlehem, to worship the Lord; and when they had opened their treasures, they presented unto him precious gifts: gold as to a mighty King, incense as to the true God, and myrrh to foreshew his burial, alleluia.

Our Father *secretly until*

℣. And lead us not into temptation.

℟. But deliver us from evil.

℣. All they from Sheba shall come.

℟. They shall bring gold and incense.

℣. O Lord, hear my prayer.

℟. And let my cry come unto thee.

℣. The Lord be with you.

℟. And with thy spirit.

Let us pray.

O GOD, who by the leading of a star didst manifest thy only-begotten Son to the Gentiles; Mercifully grant that we, who know thee now by faith, may after this life have the fruition of thy glorious Godhead. Through the same thy Son Jesus Christ our Lord, who with thee, in the unity of the Holy Spirit, liveth and reigneth God, world without end. *Amen.*

Responsory. Arise, shine, O Jerusalem, for thy light is come: and the glory of the Lord is risen upon thee, Jesus Christ, the Son of the Virgin Mary.

℣. The gentiles shall come to thy light: and kings to the brightness of thy rising.

℟. And the glory of the Lord is risen upon thee.

Let us pray.

O LORD God Almighty, bl✠ess this place (*or* this house) that here may abide health, purity, victory, strength, humility, goodness, meekness, fulfilment of the law, and giving of thanks to God the Father, the Son, and the Holy Ghost; and let thy blessing remain on this place (*or* this house) and on all who shall dwell here, now and evermore. *Amen.*

THE BLESSING OF HOUSES DURING EASTERTIDE

The Priest should be vested in surplice and white stole.

Entering the house he says,

℣. Peace be to this house.

℟. And to all that dwell in it.

Then, sprinkling with holy water the chief rooms of the house and those who dwell therein, he shall say,

Antiphon. I saw water proceeding out of the temple, from the right side thereof, alleluia: and all men, whithersoever the waters shall come, shall be healed, and shall say, alleluia, alleluia.

Ps. 118. O give thanks unto the Lord, for he is gracious, ★ because his mercy endureth forever.

Glory be to the Father, and to the Son, ★ and to the Holy Ghost;

As it was in the beginning, is now, and ever shall be, ★ world without end. Amen.

Antiphon. I saw water proceeding out of the temple, from the right side thereof, alleluia: and all men, whithersoever the waters shall come, shall be healed, and shall say, alleluia, alleluia.

℣. O Lord, show thy mercy upon us, alleluia.

℟. And grant us thy salvation, alleluia.

℣. O Lord, hear my prayer.

℟. And let my cry come unto thee.

℣. The Lord be with you.

℟. And with thy spirit.

Let us pray.

GRACIOUSLY hear us, O Lord holy, Father Almighty, everlasting God: and as at the going out from Egypt thou didst protect the houses of the

Hebrews from the destroying Angel through the sprinkling of the blood of a lamb, (figuring thereby our Passover in which Christ is sacrificed); so vouchsafe to send thy holy Angel from heaven to guard, cherish, protect, visit, and defend all who dwell in this habitation. Through the same Christ our Lord. *Amen.*

THE BLESSING OF A CEMETERY PLOT

The consecration of a cemetery is traditionally reserved to the Bishop of the Diocese or his deputy; and it is greatly to be desired that the bodies of the faithful departed in Christ be buried in consecrated ground.

In places where there are no consecrated cemeteries, the Priest may be requested to bless small burial plots of ground located in public cemeteries. The following brief service, adapted from an ancient form for consecrating a cemetery, may appropriately be used.

Vested in surplice and white stole, the Priest begins the service, saying,

Let us pray.

ALMIGHTY God, who art the keeper of all souls, and the bestower of salvation upon such as believe faithfully in thee: graciously behold this our dutiful service, and at our entry deign to make clean, to bl✠ess, and to hallow this burying place; that the bodies of those who repose therein, reunited with their souls, may be worthy to obtain eternal felicity in the great and terrible day of judgment. Through Christ our Lord. *Amen.*

He then walks once around the burial plot, sprinkling it with holy water. Meanwhile the following Antiphon and Psalm should be sung or said.

Antiphon. **Thou shalt purge me with hyssop, O Lord, and I shall be clean: thou shalt wash me, and I shall be whiter than snow.**

Psalm 51. *Miserere mei, Deus.*

HAVE mercy upon me, O God, after thy great goodness; ★ according to the multitude of thy mercies do away mine offences.

Wash me throughly from my wickedness, ★ and cleanse me from my sin.

For I acknowledge my faults, ⋆ and my sin is ever before me.

Against thee only have I sinned, and done this evil in thy sight; ⋆ that thou mightest be justified in thy saying, and clear when thou shalt judge.

Behold, I was shapen in wickedness, ⋆ and in sin hath my mother conceived me.

But lo, thou requirest truth in the inward parts, ⋆ and shalt make me to understand wisdom secretly.

Thou shalt purge me with hyssop, and I shall be clean; ⋆ thou shalt wash me, and I shall be whiter than snow.

Thou shalt make me hear of joy and gladness, ⋆ that the bones which thou hast broken may rejoice.

Turn thy face from my sins, ⋆ and put out all my misdeeds.

Make me a clean heart, O God, ⋆ and renew a right spirit within me.

Cast me not away from thy presence, ⋆ and take not thy holy Spirit from me.

O give me the comfort of thy help again, ⋆ and stablish me with thy free Spirit.

Then shall I teach thy ways unto the wicked, ⋆ and sinners shall be converted unto thee.

Deliver me from blood-guiltiness, O God, thou that art the God of my health; ⋆ and my tongue shall sing of thy righteousness.

Thou shalt open my lips, O Lord, ⋆ and my mouth shall show thy praise.

For thou desirest no sacrifice, else would I give it thee; ⋆ but thou delightest not in burnt-offerings.

The sacrifice of God is a troubled spirit; ⋆ a broken and contrite heart, O God, shalt thou not despise.

O be favourable and gracious unto Sion; ⋆ build thou the walls of Jerusalem.

Then shalt thou be pleased with the sacrifice of righteousness, with the burnt-offerings and oblations; ★ then shall they offer young bullocks upon thine altar.

Glory be to the Father, and to the Son, ★ and to the Holy Ghost;

As it was in the beginning, is now, and ever shall be, ★ world without end. Amen.

Antiphon. Thou shalt purge me with hyssop, O Lord and I shall be clean: thou shalt wash me, and I shall be whiter than snow.

Let us pray.

O GOD, who art the Creator of the whole world, and Redeemer of mankind, the righteous disposer of all thy creatures, visible and invisible: we humbly and devoutly pray thee that thou wouldst vouchsafe to make clean, hal✝low, and bless this burying place, wherein the bodies of thy servants repose after their earthly course; and forasmuch as they hoped in thee, and as thou of thy great mercy hast bestowed forgiveness of all their sins upon those who put their trust in thee, so while their bodies are at rest in this place, do thou also vouchsafe to grant thine everlasting comfort unto those who await the trump of the Archangel. Through Christ our Lord. *Amen.*

The Priest may conclude the service with the following, or he may add one or more of the Collects for the Departed, pages 89–95, as he shall think fit.

Let us pray.

O LORD Jesus Christ, who by thy death hast overcome death, and by thy rising to life again hast restored to us everlasting life: grant to all thy servants, who shall be buried in this place, that their bodies may rest in peace; and that, through the grave and gate of death, they may pass to a joyful resurrection. Who with the Father in the unity of the Holy Spirit, livest and reignest God, world without end. *Amen.*

THE blessing of God Almighty, the Father, the ✠ Son, and the Holy Ghost, be ever upon this place, and sanctify and keep it holy, that it may be a fit resting place for the bodies of his saints, until the day of the Lord Jesus, when he shall come to judge the quick and the dead. *Amen.*

And he may again sprinkle the burying ground with holy water.

Various Short Blessings

THE BLESSING OF AN ALTAR BOOK

This blessing may also be used for a prayer book or devotional manual.

℣. Our help is in the Name of the Lord.

℟. Who hath made heaven and earth.

℣. The Lord be with you.

℟. And with thy spirit.

Let us pray.

O LORD God, cause the might of thy Holy Spirit to descend upon this book, to cleanse, purify, bl✠ess, and hal✠low it: may he mercifully enlighten our hearts and give us understanding to keep thy commandments, that we may fulfil them in good works according to thy will. Through thy Son Jesus Christ our Lord, who with thee, in the unity of the same Holy Spirit, liveth and reigneth God, world without end. *Amen.*

THE BLESSING OF ALTAR CLOTHS

℣. Our help is in the Name of the Lord.

℟. Who hath made heaven and earth.

℣. The Lord be with you.

℟. And with thy spirit.

Let us pray.

O LORD, hearken unto our prayer, and vouchsafe to bl✠ess and sanc✠tify these linen cloths which are made ready for the service of thy holy Altar. Through Christ our Lord. *Amen.*

Let us pray.

O LORD God Almighty, who didst teach Moses thy servant, during forty days, to make ornaments and linen hangings, which also Miriam

wove, and made for the service of the ministry and
of the Tabernacle of Witness: be pleased to bless,
hal✠low and consecrate these linen cloths for
covering and enfolding the Altar of thy most glorious
Son Jesus Christ our Lord. Who with thee, in the
unity of the Holy Spirit, liveth and reigneth God,
world without end. *Amen.*

THE BLESSING OF A BANNER

℣. Our help is in the Name of the Lord.
℟. Who hath made heaven and earth.
℣. The Lord be with you.
℟. And with thy spirit.

Let us pray.

O LORD Jesus Christ, whose Church is as an
army set in battle array: bl✠ess this banner;
that all who are engaged in fighting under it for thee
O Lord God, may (by the intercession of blessed *N.*)
be made worthy to overcome their enemies both
visible and invisible in this world, and after victory
to triumph in the heavens. Who with the Father, in
the unity of the Holy Spirit, livest and reignest God,
world without end. *Amen.*

THE BLESSING OF CANDLES

*All candles intended for the Altar should be blessed
before use. In many places it is customary to bless the
supply for the ensuing year on February 2, using the
form on page 217. At other times the following form
should be used.*

℣. Our help is in the Name of the Lord.
℟. Who hath made heaven and earth.

℣. The Lord be with you.
℞. And with thy spirit.

Let us pray.

O LORD Jesus Christ, Son of the living God,
bl-✠-ess these candles at our supplication: pour
forth upon them O Lord, by the power of thy holy
Cr-✠-oss, thy heavenly blessing, that by them the
darkness of mankind may be dispelled; and as in
blessing they have received the sign of the holy
Cross, grant that in whatsoever places they shall be
kindled or placed, the prince of darkness with all
his hosts, trembling and afraid, may be driven out
and flee away, and presume no more to trouble or
vex those who serve thee, Almighty God. Who livest
and reignest, world without end. *Amen.*

THE BLESSING OF A CENSER

℣. Our help is in the Name of the Lord.
℞. Who hath made heaven and earth.
℣. The Lord be with you.
℞. And with thy spirit.

Let us pray.

B L-✠-ESS, we pray thee O Lord, this censer:
and grant that so often as incense is burned
therein the prayer of thy people may ascend as a
sweet-smelling savour unto thee. Through Christ our
Lord. *Amen.*

THE BLESSING OF AN ADVENT WREATH

℣. Our help is in the Name of the Lord.
℞. Who hath made heaven and earth.

℣. The Lord be with you.
℟. And with thy spirit.

Let us pray.

O LORD Jesus Christ, who art the true light that
lightest every man that cometh into the world:
bl✠ess, we pray thee, this wreath and its candles
which we shall light in preparation for thy coming;
and so enkindle our hearts with the fire of thy love
that we may receive thee with joy and gladness, and
evermore stand fast in the faith. Who livest and
reignest, world without end. *Amen.*

THE BLESSING OF THE CHRISTMAS CRIB

*In some places it is customary to use this blessing
immediately before the first, or Midnight, Mass of
Christmas. The figure of the Christ Child may rest upon
the Altar, at the Gospel side, during the Mass; afterward
it may be carried in procession to the Crib, if it be the
custom of the place.*

℣. Our help is in the Name of the Lord.
℟. Who hath made heaven and earth.
℣. The Lord be with you.
℟. And with thy spirit.

Let us pray.

A LMIGHTY and everlasting God, who as on
this night didst cause thine only begotten Son
to be born of the blessed and glorious ever virgin
Mary for our salvation: vouchsafe, we beseech thee,
so to hal✠low and bl✠ess this Crib, wherein are
shown forth the wonders of that sacred birth; that
all those who, beholding the same, shall ponder and
adore the mystery of his holy incarnation, may be

filled with thy heavenly benediction unto life eternal.
Through the same Christ our Lord. *Amen.*

THE BLESSING OF A CHURCH BELL

℣. Our help is in the Name of the Lord.
℟. Who hath made heaven and earth.
℣. Blessed be the Name of the Lord.
℟. From this time forth forevermore.
℣. The Lord be with you.
℟. And with thy spirit.

Let us pray.

A LMIGHTY God, who by thy servant Moses didst command to make two silver trumpets for the convocation of solemn assemblies: be pleased to accept our offering of this bell; bless, hal✠low, and sanctify it with thy heavenly benediction, and grant that through this generation, and through those that are to come, it may continue to call together thy faithful people to praise and worship thy holy Name. Through Christ our Lord. *Amen.*

THE BLESSING OF CORPORALS

℣. Our help is in the Name of the Lord.
℟. Who hath made heaven and earth.
℣. The Lord be with you.
℟. And with thy spirit.

Let us pray.

O MOST merciful Lord, whose power is unspeakable; whose Sacraments are celebrated with holy mysteries: grant, we beseech thee, that these linen cloths upon which the sacred Body and

Blood of our Lord Jesus Christ thy Son shall be consecrated, may be hallowed by thy favorable bene✠diction. Through the same thy Son Jesus Christ our Lord, who with thee, in the unity of the Holy Spirit, liveth and reigneth God, world without end. *Amen.*

THE BLESSING OF PALLS

℣. Our help is in the Name of the Lord.
℟. Who hath made heaven and earth.
℣. The Lord be with you.
℟. And with thy spirit.

Let us pray.

ALMIGHTY and everlasting God, be pleased to bless, hal✠low and consecrate these linen cloths for covering the Body and Blood of our Lord Jesus Christ thy Son. Who with thee, in the unity of the Holy Spirit, liveth and reigneth God, world without end. *Amen.*

THE BLESSING OF PURIFICATORS

℣. Our help is in the Name of the Lord.
℟. Who hath made heaven and earth.
℣. The Lord be with you.
℟. And with thy spirit.

Let us pray.

GRACIOUSLY hearken to our prayer, O Lord, and bl✠ess this linen prepared for use in purifying the sacred chalice. Through Christ our Lord. *Amen.*

THE BLESSING OF A MONSTRANCE

℣. Our help is in the Name of the Lord.

℟. Who hath made heaven and earth.

℣. The Lord be with you.

℟. And with thy spirit.

Let us pray.

ALMIGHTY and everlasting God, vouchsafe to bl✠ess and sanc✠tify this vessel made for exposing the Body of thy Son, our Lord Jesus Christ to the adoration of the faithful: that all who worship the same thine only-begotten with devout affection in this world, may in the world to come receive the reward of their devotion. Through the same Christ our Lord. *Amen.*

THE BLESSING OF OIL STOCKS

℣. Our help is in the Name of the Lord.

℟. Who hath made heaven and earth.

℣. The Lord be with you.

℟. And with thy spirit.

Let us pray.

HEARKEN unto our prayers, O Lord, most merciful Father: and vouchsafe to bl✠ess and sanc✠tify these oil stocks, cleansed and made ready for use in the service of thy holy Church. Through Christ our Lord. *Amen.*

Let us pray.

ALMIGHTY and everlasting God, by whom the unclean is purged, and that which is purified is made glorious: we humbly call upon thee graciously to accept these oil stocks, offered by thy servants for thy worship on earth, that by thy bl✠essing they may ever remain hallowed for the use and ministry of thy holy Church. Through Christ our Lord. *Amen.*

THE BLESSING OF ORNAMENTS FOR USE AT THE ALTAR OR IN THE CHURCH

℣. Our help is in the Name of the Lord.
℟. Who hath made heaven and earth.
℣. The Lord be with you.
℟. And with thy spirit.

Let us pray.

ALMIGHTY and everlasting God, by whom the unclean is purged, and that which is purified is made glorious: we humbly call upon thee, graciously to accept these *N.*, offered by thy servants for thy worship on earth, that by thy bl✠essing they may ever remain hallowed for the use and ministry of thy holy Church. Through Christ our Lord. *Amen.*

THE BLESSING OF A TABERNACLE, CIBORIUM, PYX, OR OTHER VESSEL FOR RESERVATION

℣. Our help is in the Name of the Lord
℟. Who hath made heaven and earth.
℣. The Lord be with you.
℟. And with thy spirit.

Let us pray.

ALMIGHTY and everlasting God, we humbly beseech thy majesty: that it may please thee to dedicate, by the grace of thy bl✠essing, this *tabernacle* made for the preserving therein of the Body of our Lord Jesus Christ. Through the same thy Son Jesus Christ our Lord, who with thee, in the unity of the Holy Spirit, liveth and reigneth God, world without end. *Amen.*

THE BLESSING OF A NEW CHURCH WINDOW

℣. Our help is in the Name of the Lord.
℟. Who hath made heaven and earth.
℣. The Lord be with you.
℟. And with thy spirit.

Let us pray.

ALMIGHTY God, who hast called us out of darkness into thy marvelous light: mercifully accept our offering of this window, which we dedicate to beautify the place of thy sanctuary, (in memory of thy servant *N.*,) and in honour of him whom thou hast given to be a light to lighten the Gentiles, Jesus Christ thy Son our Lord. Who with thee, in the unity of the Holy Spirit, liveth and reigneth God, world without end. *Amen.*

THE BLESSING OF A MEDAL

℣. Our help is in the Name of the Lord.
℟. Who hath made heaven and earth.
℣. The Lord be with you.
℟. And with thy spirit.

Let us pray.

O GOD, who didst will that two cherubim should be set upon either side of the Mercy-seat: vouchsafe, we beseech thee, of thy fatherly goodness to bl✠ess and to hal✠low this medal fashioned in honour of . . . , and grant that whosoever wears it may be kindled with devout affections, and evermore

serve thee in pureness of living. Through Jesus Christ
our Lord. *Amen.*

Or the Priest may use one of the forms on pages
137, 138.

A BRIEF BLESSING OF A MEDAL

MAY this medal be blessed in the Name of the
Father, and of the✠Son, and of the Holy
Ghost. *Amen.*

THE BLESSING OF ROSARIES

℣. Our help is in the Name of the Lord.
℞. Who hath made heaven and earth.
℣. The Lord be with you.
℞. And with thy spirit.

Let us pray.

ALMIGHTY and merciful God, who, out of the
wondrous love wherewith thou hast loved us,
that thou mightest deliver us from the power of the
evil one, didst will that thine only begotten Son, our
Lord Jesus Christ, should come down upon earth,
and at the message of an Angel take flesh from the
most holy womb of our Lady, blessed Mary, and
undergo the death of the Cross, and on the third day
rise gloriously from the dead: we implore thee
mercifully to bl✠ess and sanc✠tify *these Rosaries,*
dedicated by thy faithful Church to the honour and
praise of the same Mother of thy Son, and to so
abundantly pour forth upon *them* the power of thy
Holy Spirit that whosoever shall carry *them* about
their persons, and shall reverently keep *them* in
their houses; and shall devoutly pray unto thee,
contemplating the divine mysteries thereupon, may

abound in sound and lasting devotion, may at all times, and in all places, be delivered from every foe, visible and invisible, in this present world, and may finally at the hour of death, full of all good works, be found worthy to be presented unto thee. Through the same thy Son Jesus Christ our Lord, who with thee, in the unity of the Holy Spirit, liveth and reigneth God, world without end. *Amen.*

And he may add this prayer,

O GOD, whose only-begotten Son by his life, death, and resurrection hath purchased for us the rewards of eternal salvation: grant, we beseech thee, that meditating upon these mysteries in the holy Rosary of the blessed Virgin Mary, we may both imitate what they contain and obtain what they promise. Through the same thy Son Jesus Christ our Lord. *Amen.*

THE BRIEF FORM FOR THE BLESSING OF ROSARIES

MAY these beads of the Holy Rosary be bl✠essed and hal✠lowed, unto the praise and glory of the Virgin Mary, the Mother of God; in memory of the life, death, and resurrection of our Lord Jesus Christ: in the Name of the Father, and of the✠Son, and of the Holy Ghost. *Amen.*

THE BLESSING OF INCENSE

It is an Eastern custom for the Parish Priest to bless incense for the use of the faithful. Where such a blessing is desired, the following form will be found appropriate.

℣. Our help is in the Name of the Lord.
℟. Who hath made heaven and earth.

℣. The Lord be with you.
℟. And with thy spirit.

Let us pray.

O LORD God Almighty, in whose presence the heavenly host, whose ministrations are of spirit and fire, stand trembling: vouchsafe to behold, bl✝ess, and sanc✝tify this creature of incense, that all weakness, and all the wiles of the enemy may as its perfume ascends be put to flight, and be driven far from us, the work of thy hand, whom thou hast redeemed with the precious blood of thy Son. Hear us O Lord, for the sake of the same thy Son, Jesus Christ our Saviour. *Amen.*

THE BLESSING OF A PRIVATE ORATORY

℣. Our help is in the Name of the Lord.
℟. Who hath made heaven and earth.
℣. The Lord be with you.
℟. And with thy spirit.

Let us pray.

O GOD, who dost hallow places which are called after thy Name: pour✝thy grace upon this house of prayer, that all who here shall call upon thy holy Name may obtain the help of thy mercy. Through Christ our Lord. *Amen.*

THE BLESSING OF BREAD

℣. Our help is in the Name of the Lord.
℟. Who hath made heaven and earth.
℣. The Lord be with you.
℟. And with thy spirit.

Let us pray.

O LORD holy, Father Almighty, everlasting God, vouchsafe to bl✝ess this bread with thy spiritual benediction: that it may be to all who partake of it, health of mind and body, and a defence against all diseases and every snare of the enemy. Through thy Son Jesus Christ our Lord, the living bread, who came down from heaven and giveth life and salvation to the world; who with thee, in the unity of the Holy Spirit, liveth and reigneth God, world without end. *Amen.*

THE BLESSING OF EGGS AT EASTER

℣. Our help is in the Name of the Lord.
℞. Who hath made heaven and earth.
℣. The Lord be with you.
℞. And with thy spirit.

Let us pray.

WE beseech thee, O Lord, that the grace of thy bl✝essing may come down upon these eggs created by thee: that thy faithful people who thankfully partake of them may find them healthful food in honour of the resurrection of our Lord Jesus Christ: who with thee, in the unity of the Holy Spirit, liveth and reigneth God, world without end. *Amen.*

THE BLESSING OF A LAMB AT EASTER

℣. Our help is in the Name of the Lord.
℞. Who hath made heaven and earth.
℣. The Lord be with you.
℞. And with thy spirit.

Let us pray.

O GOD, who by thy servant Moses, when thou didst set free thy people from Egypt, didst command a lamb to be slain as a type of our Lord Jesus Christ, and didst command both the doorposts of the houses to be sprinkled with its blood: vouchsafe likewise to bl✠ess and hal✠low this flesh which we thy servants desire to receive to thy praise. Through the resurrection of the same our Lord Jesus Christ, who liveth and reigneth with thee, world without end. *Amen.*

THE BLESSING OF ANY FOOD OR MEDICINE

℣. Our help is in the Name of the Lord.

℟. Who hath made heaven and earth.

℣. The Lord be with you.

℟. And with thy spirit.

Let us pray.

B L✠ESS, O Lord, this *N.*, that it may be a wholesome remedy for mankind: and by the invocation of thy holy Name grant that whosoever shall partake thereof may receive health of body and preservation of soul. Through Christ our Lord. *Amen.*

THE BLESSING OF A FOUNDATION STONE

℣. Our help is in the Name of the Lord.

℟. Who hath made heaven and earth.

℣. The Lord be with you.

℟. And with thy spirit.

Let us pray.

O GOD, in whom every good work has its be-ginning, and going forward ever receiveth an increase of perfection: we beseech thee to grant our

petitions, that the undertaking which we have begun
to the glory of thy Name, may, being defended by
thine eternal and fatherly wisdom, be brought to a
prosperous conclusion. Through Christ our Lord.
Amen.

THE BLESSING OF A SITE OR HOUSE

℣. Our help is in the Name of the Lord.

℟. Who hath made heaven and earth.

℣. The Lord be with you.

℟. And with thy spirit.

Let us pray.

O LORD God Almighty, bl✠ess this place
(*or* this house) that here may abide health,
purity, victory, strength, humility, goodness, meekness, fulfilment of the law, and giving of thanks to
God the Father, the Son, and the Holy Ghost; and
let thy blessing remain on this place (*or* this house)
and on all who shall dwell here, now and evermore.
Amen.

*A longer form for the Blessing of a House will be
found on page* 171.

THE BLESSING OF MACHINERY

℣. Our help is in the Name of the Lord.

℟. Who hath made heaven and earth.

℣. The Lord be with you.

℟. And with thy spirit.

Let us pray.

A LMIGHTY and everlasting God, from whom
all created things do come, and by whose
marvelous providence they are ordained to serve the
use of man: bl✠ess, we humbly beseech thee, this

machine, devised to employ for our benefit the forces which thou hast made; drive far from it every snare of the enemy, and grant that those who use it may duly achieve the purpose for which it is designed, and may also ever increase in thy saving grace. Through Christ our Lord. *Amen.*

THE BLESSING OF A BRIDGE

℣. Our help is in the Name of the Lord.
℟. Who hath made heaven and earth.
℣. The Lord be with you.
℟. And with thy spirit.

Let us pray.

ASSIST us mercifully, O Lord, in these our supplications and prayers: and vouchsafe to bestow thy bl✠essing upon this bridge, that, among all the changes and chances of this mortal life, all those who pass over it may be defended by thy most gracious and ready help. Through Christ our Lord. *Amen.*

GRACIOUSLY hear us, O Lord holy, Father Almighty, everlasting God: and send thy holy Angel from heaven, to guard, protect, and defend this bridge and all who pass over it. Through Christ our Lord. *Amen.*

THE BLESSING OF SEEDS OF A FIELD

℣. Our help is in the Name of the Lord.
℟. Who hath made heaven and earth.
℣. The Lord be with you.
℟. And with thy spirit.

Let us pray.

WE pray and beseech thee, O Lord, that thou wouldst vouchsafe to bl⳨ess these seeds; to nourish them, to make them fruitful with the dew of heaven, and to bring them to fullest maturity, for the use of our bodies and souls. Through Christ our Lord. *Amen.*

THE BLESSING OF GROWING CROPS

℣. Our help is in the Name of the Lord.
℞. Who hath made heaven and earth.
℣. The Lord be with you.
℞. And with thy spirit.

Let us pray.

WE beseech thee, O Almighty God, that of thy great goodness thou wouldst vouchsafe to pour upon the first fruits of *this field* the continual dew of thy bl⳨essing: that, nourished by gentle winds and rain, the earth may bring forth her fruit in due season. Grant also that thy faithful people may show forth their thankfulness unto thee for the same by filling the hungry with the good things which the fertile earth hath brought forth, so that the poor and needy may ever praise thy glorious Name. Through Christ our Lord. *Amen.*

THE BLESSING OF THE FIRST FRUITS

A longer form will be found on page 168.

℣. Our help is in the Name of the Lord.
℞. Who hath made heaven and earth.
℣. The Lord be with you.
℞. And with thy spirit.

Let us pray.

B L✠ESS, O Lord, these new fruits of the earth, and grant that those who eat of them in thy holy Name may obtain health of mind and body. Through Christ our Lord. *Amen.*

THE BLESSING OF CATTLE AND HERDS

℣. Our help is in the Name of the Lord.

℟. Who hath made heaven and earth.

℣. The Lord be with you.

℟. And with thy spirit.

Let us pray.

O LORD God, king of heaven and earth, Word of the Father, by whom all things were made and given unto us for our use: we entreat thee mercifully to behold us thy servants. As thou dost grant us thy help in our labours and necessities, so vouchsafe of thy loving kindness and mercy to bless, keep, and protect these cattle and herds with thy heavenly bene✠diction. Grant also unto us thy servants both temporal aid and thy heavenly grace, that we may thankfully praise and glorify thy holy Name. Who with the same Father in the unity of the Holy Spirit, livest and reignest God, world without end. *Amen.*

THE BLESSING OF SICK ANIMALS

℣. Our help is in the Name of the Lord.

℟. Who hath made heaven and earth.

℣. The Lord be with you.

℟. And with thy spirit.

Let us pray.

W E humbly beseech thy mercy, O Lord, that these animals which are vexed with grave sickness may be healed in thy name, by the power of thy bene✠diction. Extinguish in them, we pray thee, all the power of the enemy; and that they may be healed of their sickness do thou, O Lord, be their defence in life, and their saving remedy. Through Christ our Lord. *Amen.*

THE BLESSING OF AN AIRPLANE

℣. Our help is in the Name of the Lord.

℟. Who hath made heaven and earth.

℣. Praise the Lord, O my soul.

℟. O my God, thou art become exceeding glorious.

℣. Who makest the clouds thy chariot.

℟. And walkest upon the wings of the wind.

℣. O Lord, hear my prayer.

℟. And let my cry come unto thee.

℣. The Lord be with you.

℟. And with thy spirit.

Let us pray.

O GOD, who hast made all things for thyself, and hast appointed every element of this world for the service of men; bl✠ess, we beseech thee, this airplane; that every evil and danger being done away, it may serve to make the praise and glory of thy holy Name more widely known, and the temporal affairs of men to be more speedily carried on; and grant that the minds of those who fly therein may cherish the desire for heavenly things. Through Christ our Lord. *Amen.*

Let us pray.

O GOD, the defender of those who trust in thee, mercifully grant unto thy servants who, journeying by air, call upon thine aid, a good Angel from

heaven to be their companion by the way: that being
kept in all their ways, they may be brought with
joy unto the haven where they would be. Through
Christ our Lord. *Amen.*

THE BLESSING OF A CARRIAGE, AUTOMOBILE, OR OTHER VEHICLE

℣. Our help is in the Name of the Lord.
℟. Who hath made heaven and earth.
℣. The Lord be with you.
℟. And with thy spirit.

Let us pray.

A SSIST us mercifully O Lord in these our supplications and prayers, and vouchsafe to bl-✝-ess
this *carriage*: give thy holy Angels charge concerning it, that all who shall ride therein may be saved
and protected from every danger. As by thy deacon
Philip thou didst give faith and grace unto the
Ethiopian eunuch as he sat in his chariot and read
thy sacred law, so now unto thy servants show the
way of salvation; that those who by the help of thy
grace are ever intent upon good works, may through
all the changes and chances of this mortal life be
made worthy to obtain eternal joys. Through Christ
our Lord. *Amen.*

THE BLESSING OF A SHIP

℣. Our help is in the Name of the Lord.
℟. Who hath made heaven and earth.
℣. The Lord be with you.
℟. And with thy spirit.

Let us pray.

BE favourable O Lord, unto our prayers, and with thy right hand bl✝ess this boat and all who shall voyage therein; stretch forth unto them thy holy arm to be their protection as thou didst stretch it forth unto blessed Peter when he walked upon the sea; and do thou send thy holy Angel from heaven to keep and deliver this vessel from every peril, together with those who voyage therein: and graciously behold thy servants, that all perils being done away, they may by a favorable course come to a fair haven; and their business ended, return rejoicing to their own homes. Who livest and reignest God, world without end. *Amen.*

THE BLESSING OF A LIFEBOAT

℣. Our help is in the Name of the Lord.

℟. Who hath made heaven and earth.

℣. The waves of the sea are mighty and rage horribly.

℟. But yet the Lord who dwelleth on high is mightier.

℣. The Lord be with you.

℟. And with thy spirit.

Let us pray.

O LORD God Almighty, who didst deliver blessed Paul thine Apostle from perils of the deep: bl✝ess, we beseech thee, this boat, that it may by thy help assist in the preservation of human life, and that those whom it rescues may ever thankfully praise thy holy Name. Through Christ our Lord. *Amen.*

THE BLESSING OF FISHING NETS

℣. Our help is in the Name of the Lord.
℟. Who hath made heaven and earth.
℣. The Lord be with you.
℟. And with thy spirit.

Let us pray.

O LORD Jesus Christ, who didst choose fishermen for thine Apostles, and didst twice grant
them a miraculous draught: bl✠ess these nets, we
pray thee, for the service of men, and grant that
those who use them may so labour in their calling
in this world, that when the net of the kingdom of
heaven is drawn to the shore they may in no wise be
cast away, but gathered into thy vessel. Through thy
mercy, O our God, who art blessed for evermore.
Amen.

THE BLESSING OF ANYTHING WHATSOEVER

℣. Our help is in the Name of the Lord.
℟. Who hath made heaven and earth.
℣. The Lord be with you.
℟. And with thy spirit.

Let us pray.

O GOD, by whose word all things are sanctified
pour thy bl✠essing upon this *N* . . . , and grant
that whosoever shall use it with thanksgiving may,
by the invocation of thy holy Name, receive from
thee, who art its maker, health of body and protection of soul. Through Christ our Lord. *Amen.*

APPENDIX

THE ASPERGES

This ancient devotion is a weekly reminder of Baptism.

Where used, it takes place on Sunday, immediately before the principal Mass. The Priest who is to celebrate, vested in a cope of the color of the Mass, and accompanied by his assistants, goes to the Altar. There, kneeling on the lowest step, he intones the antiphon, Thou shalt purge me. *And the choir continues the chant. Meanwhile he thrice sprinkles the Altar—in the midst, to his left, and to his right—and then signs himself on the forehead with holy water.*

Rising, he sprinkles his assistants, who thereupon stand up. He then sprinkles the clergy in choir (if any are present), the singers, and the congregation.

Asperges me

THOU shalt purge me with hyssop, O Lord, and I shall be clean: thou shalt wash me, and I shall be whiter than snow.

Ps. 51. Have mercy upon me, O God, after thy great goodness: ★ according to the multitude of thy mercies, do away mine offences.

Glory be to the Father, and to the Son, and to the Holy Ghost; ★ As it was in the beginning, is now and ever shall be, world without end. Amen.

Thou shalt purge me with hyssop, O Lord, and I shall be clean: thou shalt wash me, and I shall be whiter than snow.

The foregoing is sung after this order on all Sundays out of Eastertide, save that on Passion Sunday Glory be to the Father *is omitted.* Note that this devotion is omitted on Palm Sunday.

On Sundays from Easter Day through Pentecost the following antiphon is substituted for the above.

Vidi aquam

I SAW water proceeding out of the temple, from the right side thereof, alleluia: and all men, whithersoever the waters shall come, shall be healed, and shall say, alleluia, alleluia.

Ps. 118. O give thanks unto the Lord, for he is gracious, ★ because his mercy endureth forever.

Glory be to the Father and to the Son, and to the Holy Ghost; ★ As it was in the beginning, is now and ever shall be, world without end. Amen.

I saw water proceeding out of the temple, from the right side thereof, alleluia: and all men whithersoever the waters shall come, shall be healed, and shall say, alleluia, alleluia.

Having finished the antiphon after the manner prescribed above, the Priest who has sprinkled the people, standing at the foot of the Altar, sings:

℣. O Lord, show thy mercy upon us. (*in Eastertide* Alleluia *is added.*)

℞. And grant us thy salvation. (*in Eastertide* Alleluia *is added.*)

℣. O Lord hear my prayer.

℞. And let my cry come unto thee.

℣. The Lord be with you.

℞. And with thy spirit.

Let us pray.

GRACIOUSLY hear us, O Lord holy, Father Almighty, everlasting God: and send thy holy Angel from heaven to guard, cherish, protect, visit, and defend all who dwell in this habitation. Through Christ our Lord. *Amen.*

Or this:

GRACIOUSLY hear us, O Lord holy, Father Almighty, everlasting God: and vouchsafe to send thy Angel from heaven, to guard, cherish, protect, visit, and defend all who are assembled in this thy holy temple. Through Jesus Christ our Saviour. *Amen.*

The Priest then lays aside his cope, puts on the chasuble, and begins the Mass.

NOTE *that the music for the Asperges, together with the chant for the Priest, will be found fully set forth in* The Saint Dunstan Kyrial, *published by H. W. Gray Company of New York City.*

BENEDICTION OF THE BLESSED SACRAMENT

When this extra-liturgical devotion is used, it commonly follows Evening Prayer on Sundays and greater Holy Days. Occasionally it is used as a separate service. The two hymns appear in the Hymnal; the Versicle and Response are taken from the Psalter; the Collect (composed by Saint Thomas Aquinas) appears in slightly varying translations in official Prayer Books of the Anglican Communion, and in the Book of Offices set forth by the House of Bishops of the American Church. The Divine Praises were originally said in reparation for profane language.

If this devotion takes place immediately after Solemn Evensong, the Priest wears stole and cope of the color of the day over his surplice; at other times the stole and cope should be white. The humeral veil should always be white. On the Altar, extra candles should be lighted as for a festival. The monstrance, covered with a veil, should be on the Altar before the service begins, together with a white burse containing a corporal. This corporal should be used only at Benediction.

The Priest and his assistants approach the Altar, genuflect, and kneel on the lowest step. After a brief prayer, the Priest stands, goes up to the Altar, and there spreads the corporal. He uncovers the monstrance, unlocks and opens the tabernacle, and genuflects. Then taking the case which contains the sacred Host from its receptacle, he places it securely in the monstrance. The hymn O salutaris hostia *is begun at once. Taking care that the monstrance faces the congregation, the Priest genuflects, goes to the lowest step, and kneels. Then the Priest, standing at the foot of the Altar, puts incense in the censer, (without blessing it, since only the Blessed Sacrament is to be censed); and, kneeling on the lowest step, he censes the Blessed Sacrament with three double swings, bowing his head profoundly before and afterwards.*

O salutaris hostia

O SAVING Victim, opening wide
The gate of heaven to man below,
Our foes press on from every side,
Thine aid supply, thy strength bestow.

All praise and thanks to thee ascend
For evermore, blest One in Three;
O grant us life that shall not end,
In our true native land with thee. Amen.

*A Litany or hymn of praise may here be sung, or
some devotion appropriate to the time; e.g., the Te Deum
(all standing) on great feasts or occasions of public
rejoicing, or the Penitential Office on Ash Wednesday.*

*During the second line of the following hymn, all
should humbly bow; at the beginning of the second
stanza incense is offered as before.*

Tantum ergo Sacramentum

T HEREFORE we before him bending,
This great Sacrament revere;
Types and shadows have their ending,
For the newer rite is here;
Faith, our outward sense befriending,
Makes our inward vision clear.

Glory let us give and blessing
To the Father and the Son;
Honour, thanks, and praise addressing,
While eternal ages run;
Ever too his love confessing
Who, from both, with both is one. Amen.

Still kneeling, the Priest sings:

℣. Thou gavest them bread from heaven.
(Alleluia†.)

℟. Containing in itself all sweetness.
(Alleluia.)

Let us pray.

O GOD, who in a wonderful Sacrament hast left unto us a memorial of thy Passion: grant us, we beseech thee, so to venerate the sacred mysteries of thy Body and Blood, that we may ever perceive within ourselves the fruit of thy redemption. Who livest and reignest, world without end. *Amen.*

Kneeling, the Priest receives the humeral veil on his shoulders. Then he goes up to the Altar, genuflects, takes the monstrance into his hands, holding it with the ends of the veil. Turning by his right to the people, the Priest gives the Blessing (or Benediction) *in silence, making the sign of the Cross with the monstrance over the kneeling congregation. Meanwhile an acolyte rings the sanctus bell thrice; and the thurifer censes the Blessed Sacrament with three double swings.*

Turning back to the Altar by his right, the Priest places the monstrance on the Altar, genuflects, and goes to kneel at the foot of the Altar, where he leads the congregation in reciting

THE DIVINE PRAISES

Blessed be God.
Blessed be his holy Name.

---

†NOTE *that* Alleluia *should be added to the Versicle and Response, and to the Antiphon, in Eastertide, and on the feast of Corpus Christi.*

Blessed be Jesus Christ, true God and true man.
Blessed be the Name of Jesus.
Blessed be his most sacred Heart.
Blessed be his most precious Blood.
Blessed be Jesus in the most holy Sacrament of the Altar.
Blessed be the Holy Spirit, the Comforter.
Blessed be the great Mother of God, Mary most holy.
Blessed be the name of Mary, Virgin and Mother,
Blessed be Saint Joseph her most chaste spouse.
Blessed be God in his Angels and in his Saints.

The Priest rises, goes to the Altar, genuflects, and removing the case containing the sacred Host from the monstrance, puts it back into its receptacle. This is replaced in the tabernacle. The Priest genuflects, closes and locks the tabernacle, puts the corporal back into its burse, veils the monstrance, and goes to stand at the foot of the Altar.

As soon as the Priest has replaced the Blessed Sacrament in the tabernacle, all rise and sing:

Antiphon. **Let us for ever adore: the most holy Sacrament. (Alleluia.)**

Psalm 117. *Laudate Dominum.*

O PRAISE the Lord, all ye nations ★ praise him, all ye peoples.

For his merciful kindness is ever more and more toward us ★ and the truth of the Lord endureth for ever. Praise the Lord.

Glory be to the Father, and to the Son, ★ and to the Holy Ghost.

As it was in the beginning, is now, and ever shall be, ★ world without end. Amen.

Antiphon. Let us for ever adore: the most holy Sacrament. (Alleluia.)

The Priest and his assistants may leave the Sanctuary after the first half of Glory be to the Father *has been sung.*

BENEDICTION WITH THE CIBORIUM

The preceding service is used, with the following variations:

The Priest is vested in surplice and white stole. He need not wear a cope.

Arriving at the Altar, the Priest spreads the corporal before the tabernacle, then he unlocks and opens the tabernacle, genuflects, and leaves it open, so that the people may see the ciborium. He does not place the ciborium upon the Altar.

If incense is used, the Blessed Sacrament is censed at the usual times.

For the blessing, the Priest receives the humeral veil as usual, goes up to the Altar, genuflects, takes the ciborium and places it on the corporal before the tabernacle. He takes it with the right hand covered by the veil, and arranges the other end of the veil over the ciborium. He turns and gives the blessing, (or Benediction) *with the ciborium, making one sign of the Cross. He then replaces the ciborium in the tabernacle, and genuflects.*

After the Divine Praises have been said, the Priest closes and locks the tabernacle.

THE BLESSING AND DISTRIBUTION OF CANDLES ON FEBRUARY 2

This ancient blessing, symbolic of Christ the True Light of the world, should take place immediately before the principal Mass on the Feast of the Purification. In many places it is customary to bless the year's supply of candles together with the candles which are to be given to the people at this service.

The candles to be blessed and distributed are usually placed at the Epistle side of the Sanctuary, near the Altar. The Altar should be vested in white. The Priest who is to celebrate, vested in amice, alb, girdle, white stole and cope (if no cope is available the chasuble may be worn), having arrived at the Altar, goes to the Epistle side. Without turning to the people, he begins the office of blessing, singing or saying:

℣. **The Lord be with you.**
℟. **And with thy spirit.**

Let us pray.

ALMIGHTY **and everlasting God, who as on this day didst present thine only-begotten Son in thy holy temple to be received in the arms of blessed Simeon: we humbly entreat thy mercy, that thou wouldst vouchsafe to bl-☩-ess, hal-☩-low, and kindle with the light of thy heavenly benediction these candles which we thy servants desire to receive and to carry, lighted in honor of thy holy Name. By offering them to thee our Lord and God, may we be inflamed with the fire of thy love, and made worthy to be presented in the holy temple of thy glory. Through the same thy Son Jesus Christ our Lord, who with thee, in the unity of the Holy Spirit, liveth and reigneth God, world without end.** *Amen.*

*Then the Priest, after putting incense into the thurible
and blessing it, will thrice sprinkle the candles with holy
water, saying once only,*

**Thou shalt purge me with hyssop O Lord, and I
shall be clean: thou shalt wash me, and I shall be
whiter than snow.** *Then he censes them thrice.*

*If another Priest is present, he gives a candle to the
celebrant, who does not kneel. Other clergy and acolytes
receive their candles kneeling at the footpace; the people
kneel at the Altar Rail.*

During the distribution it is customary to sing the
Nunc dimittis, *in the following manner:*

Lumen ad revelationem

A LIGHT to lighten the Gentiles: and the glory
of thy people Israel.

L ORD, now lettest thou thy servant depart in
peace ★ according to thy word.
A light to lighten the Gentiles: and the glory of
thy people Israel.
For mine eyes have seen ★ thy salvation.
A light to lighten the Gentiles: and the glory of
thy people Israel.
Which thou hast prepared ★ before the face of all
people.
A light to lighten the Gentiles: and the glory of
thy people Israel.
To be a light to lighten the Gentiles ★ and to be
the glory of thy people Israel.
A light to lighten the Gentiles: and the glory of
thy people Israel.
Glory be to the Father, and to the Son, ★ and to
the Holy Ghost.

A light to lighten the Gentiles: and the glory of thy people Israel.

As it was in the beginning, is now and ever shall be, ✶ world without end. Amen.

A light to lighten the Gentiles: and the glory of thy people Israel.

When all have received their candles, and returned to their places, the candles which the people are carrying should be lighted. The light may be given by acolytes or ushers. As soon as the anthem is finished, the Priest shall sing or say:

Let us pray.

WE beseech thee, O Lord, mercifully to hear the prayers of thy people: and grant that by this service which year by year we offer unto thee, we may attain in the light of thy grace to the hidden things of thy glory. Through Christ our Lord. *Amen.*

Then the Procession is formed. And first the Priest puts incense in the censer and blesses it; turning to the people he sings,

Let us go forth in peace.

The choir and people answer,

In the Name of Christ. Amen.

During the Procession, all carry lighted candles, and appropriate hymns and anthems should be sung.

The Procession ended, the Priest lays aside his cope, and puts on the chasuble for the Mass of the feast. It is an ancient custom for all to hold lighted candles during the reading of the Gospel, and from the Consecration to the Communion.

THE BLESSING AND IMPOSITION OF ASHES ON THE FIRST DAY OF LENT

This ancient blessing, which gave its distinctive title to Ash Wednesday, is a reminder of our common mortality, and of our need for corporate penance.

Traditionally, the ashes are of palms blessed and used on the preceding Palm Sunday. The ashes to be blessed should be in some fitting vessel on the Epistle side of the Altar. Note that the ashes should be powdered and dry.

Immediately before Mass, the Priest who is to celebrate, vested in amice, alb, girdle, violet stole and cope (if no cope is available the chasuble may be worn), having arrived at the Altar, goes to the Epistle side. He reads the following Antiphon, or it may be sung by the choir.

Exaudi nos

HEAR us, O Lord, for thy loving-kindness is comfortable: according to the multitude of thy mercies, turn thee unto us, O Lord.

Ps. 69. Save me, O God, for the waters are come in, ⋆ even unto my soul.

Glory be to the Father and to the Son, and to the Holy Ghost; ⋆ As is it was in the beginning, is now, and ever shall be, world without end. Amen.

Hear us, O Lord, for thy loving-kindness is comfortable: according to the multitude of thy mercies, turn thee unto us, O Lord.

Without turning to the people, the Priest sings or says:

℣. The Lord be with you.
℟. And with thy spirit.

Let us pray.

O GOD, who desirest not the death of a sinner,
but rather that he should turn from his sin
and be saved: mercifully look upon the frailty of
our mortal nature, and of thy goodness vouchsafe
to bl✛ess these ashes now to be set upon our heads
in token of humility and to obtain thy pardon; that
we, knowing we are but dust, and that for our unworthiness unto dust shall we return, may through
thy mercy be found meet to receive forgiveness of
all our sins, and those good things which thou hast
promised to the penitent. Through Christ our Lord.
Amen.

*Then the Priest, after putting incense into the thurible
and blessing it, will thrice sprinkle the ashes with holy
water, saying once only,*

Thou shalt purge me with hyssop, O Lord, and I
shall be clean: thou shalt wash me and I shall be
whiter than snow. *Then he censes them thrice.*

*If another Priest is present, he gives the ashes to the
Celebrant, who does not kneel. If no other Priest is
present, the Celebrant, standing, puts ashes on his own
head, saying nothing. Other clergy and acolytes receive
the ashes kneeling at the footpace, the people kneel at
the Altar Rail. Meanwhile appropriate hymns or anthems
may be sung.*

*In giving the ashes it is customary for the Priest,
dipping his thumb in the ashes, to make the sign of the
cross on the peoples' foreheads, saying,*

R EMEMBER O man, that dust thou art, and
unto dust shalt thou return.

When all have received the ashes, the Priest washes his hands. Standing at the Epistle side of the Altar he sings or says,

℣. **The Lord be with you.**

℟. **And with thy spirit.**

Let us pray.

GRANT us, O Lord, to begin with holy fasting this campaign of our Christian warfare: that as we do battle with spiritual wickedness we may be defended by the aids of self-denial. Through Christ our Lord. *Amen.*

Having said this prayer, the Priest changes his cope for the chasuble, and begins the Mass.

NOTE. *By ancient custom, the Priest who officiates at this blessing should always celebrate the Mass which follows.*

Ashes once blessed may be imposed at any time in the course of the day.

THE BLESSING OF PALMS
ON THE SUNDAY NEXT BEFORE EASTER

This blessing, from which the Sunday Next Before Easter derives its common name of Palm Sunday, takes place on that day, immediately before the principal Mass. According to the very ancient custom of the Church, the Priest who blesses the palms should always celebrate the Mass which follows.

The Palms to be blessed should be placed on a table set in the midst of the Sanctuary or Chancel, where it can be seen by the people.

Where there is no choir, that which is appointed to be sung in this office may be read without note.

The Altar is vested in red over violet in honour of Christ the King of Martyrs; the Priest is vested in amice, alb, girdle, red stole and cope. If no cope is available, he may wear a chasuble.

As the Priest and his assistants approach the Altar, the choir sings:

HOSANNA to the Son of David: blessed is he that cometh in the Name of the Lord. O King of Israel: Hosanna in the highest.

The Priest stands behind the table, facing the people. He sings:

℣. The Lord be with you.
℟. And with thy spirit.

Let us pray.

BL✠ESS, O Lord, we beseech thee, these branches of the palm tree: and grant that what thy people today show forth corporally for thy honour, they may perform spiritually with great devotion; and by ardently loving good works, may at last gain the victory over their enemy. Through thy Son Jesus Christ our Lord, who with thee, in the unity of the Holy Spirit, liveth and reigneth God, world without end. *Amen.*

The Priest puts incense into the thurible, and then sprinkles the branches thrice with holy water, saying once only, Thou shalt purge me with hyssop, O Lord, and I shall be clean: thou shalt wash me and I shall be whiter than snow. *Then he censes them thrice.*

Then the Celebrant distributes the palms. Clergy and acolytes receive their branches kneeling at the footpace; the people kneel at the Altar Rail.

Meanwhile the choir may sing appropriate hymns and anthems.

After the distribution, the Priest washes his hands, and the table is removed.

Then the Priest goes up to the Altar and kisses it. He blesses incense, and proceeds to the singing of the Gospel, in the accustomed manner. At the end he kisses the book, but is not censed.

✠ *The Holy Gospel.* Saint Matthew 21. 1.

WHEN they drew nigh unto Jerusalem, and were come to Bethphage, unto the mount of Olives, then sent Jesus two disciples, saying unto them, Go into the village over against you, and straightway ye shall find an ass tied, and a colt with her: loose them, and bring them unto me. And if any man say ought unto you, ye shall say, The Lord hath need of them; and straightway he will send them. All this was done, that it might be fulfilled which was spoken by the prophet, saying, Tell ye the daughter of Sion, Behold, thy King cometh unto thee, meek, and sitting upon an ass, and a colt the foal of an ass. And the disciples went, and did as Jesus commanded them, and brought the ass, and the colt, and put on them their clothes, and they set him thereon. And a very great multitude spread their garments in the way; others cut down branches from the trees, and strawed them in the way. And the multitudes that went before, and that followed, cried, saying, Hosanna to the son of David: Blessed is he that cometh in the name of the Lord, Hosanna in the highest.

Then the Procession is formed. And first the Celebrant puts incense in the censer and blesses it; turning to the people, he sings

Let us go forth in peace.

The choir and people answer,

In the Name of Christ. Amen.

The Procession begins. First goes the thurifer, bearing the censer, then the crucifer carrying an unveiled cross, between two servers with lighted candles. Other servers and the clergy follow according to rank. In some places it is customary for the people to follow the Celebrant.

During the Procession, all carry palm branches; and appropriate hymns or anthems may be sung.

As the Procession goes forward, the following hymn is sung, all the people repeating the first verse, as noted.

Gloria, laus, et honor

ALL **glory, laud, and honour to thee, Redeemer, King!**
To whom the lips of children made sweet hosannas ring.

℟. **All glory, laud, and honour.**

Thou art the King of Israel, thou David's royal Son:
Who in the Lord's Name comest, the King and
Blessed One.

R̲. All glory, laud, and honour.

The company of Angels are praising thee on high,
And mortal men and all things created make reply.

R̲. All glory, laud, and honour.

The people of the Hebrews with palms before thee
went:
Our praise and prayers and anthems before thee
we present.

R̲. All glory, laud, and honour.

To thee before thy Passion they sang their hymns of
praise:
To thee now high exalted our melody we raise.

R̲. All glory, laud, and honour.

Thou didst accept their praises, accept the prayers
we bring:
Who in all good delightest, thou good and gracious
King.

R̲. All glory, laud, and honour.

*Arrived in the Sanctuary, the Priest goes up to the
Altar, kisses it, and turning to the people sings:*

V̲. The Lord be with you.
R̲. And with thy spirit.

Let us pray.

O LORD Jesus Christ, our King and our Redeemer, in whose honour we have carried these
branches while chanting thy solemn praises: mercifully grant; that thy grace and heavenly benediction

may descend wheresoever these branches shall be taken, and by thy mighty power defend those whom thou hast redeemed from all assaults of the enemy. Who with the Father, in the unity of the Holy Spirit, livest and reignest God, world without end. *Amen.*

Then the Priest goes to the sedilia, removes his red cope and stole, and puts on the violet stole and chasuble. Meanwhile the red Altar hangings are removed, exposing the violet beneath, and the Altar is made ready for Mass.

As the choir begins the Introit the Priest goes to the foot of the Altar, makes the accustomed reverence, and, omitting the Preparation, goes up to the footpace.

SOLEMN BAPTISM

*The Priest is ordinarily vested in surplice and violet
stole; if he be administering this Sacrament during the
Liturgy of the Easter Vigil, he will be vested in amice,
alb, girdle, violet stole and cope.*

HATH this Child (Person) been already baptized
or no?

If the Godparents answer, No: *then shall the Priest
proceed as followeth.*

DEARLY beloved, forasmuch as our Saviour
Christ saith, None can enter into the kingdom
of God, except he be regenerate and born anew of
Water and of the Holy Ghost; I beseech you to
call upon God the Father, through our Lord Jesus
Christ, that of his bounteous mercy he will grant to
this Child (*this person*) that which by nature *he*
cannot have; that *he* may be baptized with Water
and the Holy Ghost, and received into Christ's holy
Church and be made *a* living *member* of the same.

Then shall the Priest say,

Let us pray.

ALMIGHTY and immortal God, the aid of all
who need, the helper of all who flee to thee for
succour, the life of those who believe, and the
resurrection of the dead; We call upon thee for
this Child (*this* thy *Servant*), that *he*, coming to
thy holy Baptism, may receive remission of sin, by
spiritual regeneration. Receive *him*, O Lord, as thou
hast promised by thy well-beloved Son, saying, Ask,
and ye shall have; seek, and ye shall find; knock,
and it shall be opened unto you. So give now unto
us who ask; let us who seek, find; open the gate
unto us who knock; that *this Child* (*this* thy *Servant*)

228

may enjoy the everlasting benediction of thy heavenly
washing, and may come to the eternal kingdom
which thou hast promised by Christ our Lord.
Amen.

*If it is so desired, the Priest then takes a few grains
of hallowed salt between his right thumb and index
finger, and placing the salt in the mouth of the person to
be baptized, says,*

RECEIVE the salt of wisdom: may it be unto
thee a pledge of everlasting life. *Amen.*

℣. The Lord be with you.
℟. And with thy spirit.

Hear ✠ the words ✠ of the Gospel ✠, written
by Saint Mark, in the tenth Chapter, at the thirteenth
Verse.

℟. Glory be to thee, O Lord.

THEY brought young children to Christ, that he
should touch them: and his disciples rebuked
those that brought them. But when Jesus saw it, he
was much displeased, and said unto them, Suffer
the little children to come unto me, and forbid them
not: for of such is the kingdom of God. Verily I say
unto you, Whosoever shall not receive the kingdom
of God as a little child, he shall not enter therein.
And he took them up in his arms, put his hands
upon them, and blessed them.

℟. Praise be to thee, O Christ.

Or this.

℣. The Lord be with you.
℟. And with thy spirit.

Hear ✠ the words ✠ of the Gospel ✠, written
by Saint John, in the third Chapter, at the first
Verse.

℞. Glory be to thee, O Lord.

THERE was a man of the Pharisees, named
Nicodemus, a ruler of the Jews: the same came
to Jesus by night, and said unto him, Rabbi, we know
that thou art a teacher come from God: for no man
can do these miracles that thou doest, except God
be with him. Jesus answered and said unto him,
Verily, verily, I say unto thee, Except a man be
born again, he cannot see the kingdom of God.
Nicodemus said unto him, How can a man be born
when he is old? can he enter the second time into
his mother's womb, and be born? Jesus answered,
Verily, verily, I say unto thee, Except a man be
born of water and of the Spirit, he cannot enter into
the kingdom of God. That which is born of the flesh
is flesh; and that which is born of the Spirit is spirit.
Marvel not that I said unto thee, Ye must be born
again. The wind bloweth where it listeth, and thou
hearest the sound thereof, but canst not tell whence
it cometh, and whither it goeth: so is every one that
is born of the Spirit.

℞. Praise be to thee, O Christ.

Or this.

℣. The Lord be with you.
℞. And with thy spirit.

Hear ✠ the words ✠ of the Gospel ✠, written
by Saint Matthew, in the twenty-eighth Chapter, at
the eighteenth Verse.

℞. Glory be to thee, O Lord.

JESUS came and spake unto them, saying, All power is given unto me in heaven and in earth. Go ye therefore, and make disciples of all nations, baptizing them in the name of the Father, and of the Son, and of the Holy Ghost: teaching them to observe all things whatsoever I have commanded you: and, lo, I am with you alway, even unto the end of the world.

℟. Praise be to thee, O Christ.

Then shall the Priest say,

AND now, being persuaded of the good will of our heavenly Father toward *this Child (this Person)*, declared by his Son Jesus Christ; let us faithfully and devoutly give thanks unto him, and say,

Priest and People.

ALMIGHTY and everlasting God, heavenly Father, We give thee humble thanks, That thou hast vouchsafed to call us To the knowledge of thy grace, and faith in thee: Increase this knowledge, And confirm this faith in us evermore. Give thy Holy Spirit to *this Child (this* thy *Servant)*, That *he* may be born again, And be made *an heir* of everlasting salvation; Through our Lord Jesus Christ, Who liveth and reigneth with thee and the same Holy Spirit, Now and for ever. Amen.

When the office is used for a Child, the Priest shall speak unto the Godparents on this wise.

DEARLY beloved, ye have brought *this Child* here to be baptized; ye have prayed that our Lord Jesus Christ would vouchsafe to receive *him*, to release *him* from sin, to sanctify *him* with the

Holy Ghost, to give *him* the kingdom of heaven, and everlasting life.

Dost thou, therefore, in the name of this Child, renounce the devil and all his works, the vain pomp and glory of the world, with all covetous desires of the same, and the sinful desires of the flesh, so that thou wilt not follow, nor be led by them?

Answer. I renounce them all; and, by God's help, will endeavour not to follow, nor be led by them.

According to ancient custom, the Priest here anoints the Child with the Oil of the Catechumens, on the breast (at the base of the neck) and on the back between the shoulders, in the form of a Cross, saying once only:

I anoint thee with the Oil ✠ of salvation, in Christ ✠ Jesus our Lord, that thou mayest have eternal life.

If the water has already been blessed, the Priest here changes his stole (and cope) from violet to white, and continues:

Priest. Dost thou believe all the Articles of the Christian Faith, as contained in the Apostles' Creed?
Answer. I do.

Priest. Wilt thou be baptized in this Faith?
Answer. That is my desire.

Priest. Wilt thou then obediently keep God's holy will and commandments, and walk in the same all the days of thy life?
Answer. I will, by God's help.

Priest. Having now, in the name of this Child, made these promises, wilt thou also on thy part take heed that this Child learn the Creed, the Lord's Prayer, and the Ten Commandments, and all other things which a Christian ought to know and believe to his soul's health?

Answer. I will, by God's help.

Priest. Wilt thou take heed that this Child, so soon as sufficiently instructed, be brought to the Bishop to be confirmed by him?

Answer. I will, God being my helper.

When the Office is used for an Adult, the Priest shall address him on this wise, the Person answering the questions for himself.

WELL - BELOVED, you have come hither desiring to receive holy Baptism. We have prayed that our Lord Jesus Christ would vouchsafe to receive you, to release you from sin, to sanctify you with the Holy Ghost, to give you the kingdom of heaven, and everlasting life.

DOST thou renounce the devil and all his works, the vain pomp and glory of the world, with all covetous desires of the same, and the sinful desires of the flesh, so that thou wilt not follow, nor be led by them?

Answer. I renounce them all; and, by God's help, will endeavour not to follow, nor be led by them.

Here the Priest may anoint the Person with the Oil of the Catechumens on the breast (at the base of the neck) and on the back between the shoulders, in the form of a Cross, saying once only:

I anoint thee with the Oil ✠ of salvation, in Christ ✠ Jesus our Lord, that thou mayest have eternal life.

If the water has already been blessed, the Priest here changes his stole (and cope) from violet to white, and continues:

Priest. **Dost thou believe in Jesus the Christ, the Son of the Living God?**

Answer. **I do.**

Priest. **Dost thou accept him, and desire to follow him as thy Saviour and Lord?**

Answer. **I do.**

Priest. **Dost thou believe all the Articles of the Christian Faith, as contained in the Apostles Creed?**

Answer. **I do.**

Priest. **Wilt thou be baptized in this Faith?**

Answer. **That is my desire.**

Priest. **Wilt thou then obediently keep God's holy will and commandments, and walk in the same all the days of thy life?**

Answer. **I will, by God's help.**

Then shall the Priest say,

O MERCIFUL God, grant that like as Christ died and rose again, so *this Child* (*this* thy *Servant*) may die to sin and rise to newness of life. *Amen.*

Grant that all sinful affections may die in *him*, and that all things belonging to the Spirit may live and grow in *him*. *Amen.*

Grant that *he* may have power and strength to have victory, and to triumph, against the devil, the world, and the flesh. *Amen.*

Grant that whosoever is here dedicated to thee by our office and ministry, may also be endued with

heavenly virtues, and everlastingly rewarded, through thy mercy, O blessed Lord God, who dost live, and govern all things, world without end. *Amen.*

If the water has already been solemnly blessed, as on the Easter Vigil, the Priest omits that which follows, and goes at once to Name this Child, *on page* 236.

℣. The Lord be with you.

℟. And with thy spirit.

℣. Lift up your hearts.

℟. We lift them up unto the Lord.

℣. Let us give thanks unto our Lord God.

℟. It is meet and right so to do.

Then the Priest shall say,

IT is very meet, right, and our bounden duty, that we should give thanks unto thee, O Lord, Holy Father, Almighty, Everlasting God, for that thy dearly beloved Son Jesus Christ, for the forgiveness of our sins, did shed out of his most precious side both water and blood; and gave commandment to his disciples, that they should go teach all nations, and baptize them In the Name of the Father, and of the Son, and of the Holy Ghost. Regard, we beseech thee, the supplications of thy congregation; sanc-✠tify this Water to the mystical washing away of sin; and grant that *this Child* (*this* thy *Servant*), now to be baptized therein, may receive the fulness of thy grace, and ever remain in the number of thy faithful children; through the same Jesus Christ our Lord, to whom, with thee, in the unity of the Holy Spirit, be all honour and glory, now and evermore. *Amen.*

If he has not already done so, the Priest here changes his stole (and cope) from violet to white.

Then the Priest shall take the Child into his arms, and shall say to the Godfathers and Godmothers,

Name this Child.

And then, naming the Child after them, he shall dip him in the Water discreetly, or shall pour Water upon him, saying,

N. I baptize thee In the Name of the Father, and of the Son, and of the Holy Ghost. Amen.

But NOTE, *That if the Person to be baptized be an Adult, the Priest shall take him by the hand, and shall ask the Witnesses the Name; and then shall dip him in the Water, or pour Water upon him, using the same form of words.*

But if the Baptism be Conditional, he shall use the following form:

IF thou art not already baptized, *N.,* I baptize thee In the Name of the Father, and of the Son, and of the Holy Ghost. Amen.

Then the Priest shall say,

WE receive this Child (Person) into the congregation of Christ's flock; and do ★ sign *him* with the sign of the Cross, in token that hereafter *he* shall not be ashamed to confess the faith of Christ crucified, and manfully to fight under his

* *Here the Priest shall make a Cross upon the Child's (or Person's) forehead, (using the holy Chrism, if desired).*

banner, against sin, the world, and the devil; and to continue Christ's faithful soldier and servant unto *his* life's end. Amen.

Or, having signed the Child or Person with the Cross in the usual manner, the Priest may then anoint him *upon the crown of the head with the holy Chrism, saying,*

ALMIGHTY God, the Father of our Lord Jesus Christ, who hath regenerated thee by Water and the Holy Ghost, and hath given unto thee remission of all thy sins, vouchsafe to an✝oint thee with the Unction of his Holy Spirit, and bring thee to the inheritance of everlasting life. *Amen.*

If it is so desired, the Priest shall put upon the Child *the white vesture commonly called the Chrysom, saying,*

WE give this white vesture, for a token of the innocency bestowed upon thee, and for a sign whereby thou art admonished to give thyself to pureness of living, that after this transitory life thou mayest be partaker of the life everlasting. *Amen.*

Then the Priest may give him *a lighted candle, (in the case of an Infant, the candle should be given to the Godfather), saying.*

RECEIVE the light of Christ, that when the bridegroom cometh thou mayest go forth with all the Saints to meet him; and see that thou keep the grace of thy Baptism. *Amen.*

Then shall the Priest say,

SEEING now, dearly beloved brethren, that *this Child (this Person) is* regenerate, and grafted into the body of Christ's Church, let us give thanks unto Almighty God for these benefits; and with one accord make our prayers unto him, that *this Child (this Person)* may lead the rest of *his* life according to this beginning.

Then shall be said,

OUR Father, who art in heaven, Hallowed be thy Name. Thy kingdom come. Thy will be done, On earth as it is in heaven. Give us this day our daily bread. And forgive us our trespasses, As we forgive those who trespass against us. And lead us not into temptation, But deliver us from evil. For thine is the kingdom, and the power, and the glory, for ever and ever. Amen.

Then shall the Priest say,

WE yield thee hearty thanks, most merciful Father, that it hath pleased thee to regenerate *this Child (this* thy *Servant)* with thy Holy Spirit, to receive *him* for thine own *Child,* and to incorporate *him* into thy holy Church. And humbly we beseech thee to grant, that *he,* being dead unto sin, may live unto righteousness, and being buried with Christ in his death, may also be *partaker* of his resurrection; so that finally, with the residue of thy holy Church, *he* may be *an inheritor* of thine everlasting kingdom; through Christ our Lord. *Amen.*

Then the Priest shall add,

THE Almighty God, the Father of our Lord Jesus Christ, of whom the whole family in heaven and earth is named; Grant you to be strengthened with might by his Spirit in the inner man; that, Christ dwelling in your hearts by faith, ye may be filled with all the fulness of God. *Amen.*

NOTE ON THE CEREMONIES

THE ceremonies suggested for use in the solemn administration of Holy Baptism have come down to us from the earliest ages. The Imposition of Salt appears in the English Manuals. The form for the anointing with the Oil of the Catechumens is taken from the York Manual; that for anointing with the holy Chrism from the First Prayer Book of Edward VI. The forms for the giving of the Chrysom and the lighted candle are supplied from the Occasional Offices of the Church of the Province of South Africa. The use of the holy Chrism at "We receive this *child*" was suggested by the English Church Union at the time of the last revision of the English Prayer Book.

THE CONSECRATION OF A CHALICE AND PATEN

This blessing is traditionally reserved to the Bishop of the Diocese, or to another Bishop delegated by him. The Bishop should be vested in rochet, stole, and mitre. He should be attended by at least two chaplains; one of whom will minister the holy Chrism.

Standing, and wearing his mitre, the Bishop begins the blessing, saying,

℣. Our help is in the Name of the Lord.

℟. Who hath made heaven and earth.

LET us pray, dearly beloved brethren, that the blessing of divine grace may consecrate and hallow this Paten (*or* these Patens) for the consecration of the Body of our Lord Jesus Christ, who endured the sufferings of the Cross for our salvation, and for that of all men.

Then the Bishop lays aside his mitre and says,

℣. The Lord be with you.

℟. And with thy spirit.

Let us pray.

ALMIGHTY and everlasting God, who didst ordain the sacrifices of the law, and who didst command that among the rest wheaten cakes should be borne on plates of gold and silver to thine Altar: be pleased to bless, hal-✠-low, and consecrate this Paten (*or* these Patens) for the administration of the Eucharist of Jesus Christ thy Son, who for our salvation, and for that of all men, willed to offer his very self unto thee, O God the Father, upon the gibbet of the Cross; who with thee, in the unity of the Holy Spirit, liveth and reigneth God, world without end. *Amen.*

240

The Bishop puts on the mitre. He dips the tip of his right thumb in the holy Chrism, and proceeds to anoint the Paten or Patens. First he makes the sign of the Cross upon each Paten, signing it from edge to edge. Then, rubbing gently with the same thumb, he anoints the whole upper surface of each Paten, saying,

O LORD God, be pleased to consecrate and hallow this Paten by this anointing, and by our bene✠diction in Christ Jesus our Lord: Who with thee in the unity of the Holy Spirit, liveth and reigneth God, world without end. *Amen.*

Next, standing and wearing the mitre, he proceeds to bless the Chalice, saying,

LET us pray, dearly beloved brethren, that the Lord our God may hallow this chalice (*or* these Chalices) to be consecrated for the service of his ministry, by the inspiration of his heavenly grace; and that he may be pleased to accompany this consecration by man with the fulness of his heavenly favour. Through Christ our Lord. *Amen.*

Then, laying aside his mitre, he says,

℣. The Lord be with you.
℟. And with thy spirit.

Let us pray.

O LORD our God, be pleased to bl✠ess this Chalice (*or* these Chalices), prepared for the use of thy ministry by the loving devotion of thy servants, and pour upon *it* that sanctification of thine, which thou didst pour upon the sacred Chalice of Melchizedek thy servant; and although neither in precious metal nor by human skill can anything be made worthy of thine Altars, yet do thou grant

that this Chalice (*or* these Chalices) may be made
holy by thy benediction. Through Christ our Lord.
Amen.

*The Bishop puts on the mitre. He dips the tip of his
right thumb in the holy Chrism, and proceeds to anoint
the inside of the cup. First he makes the sign of the Cross
in the cup, signing it from lip to lip. Then, rubbing
gently with the same thumb, he anoints the whole inner
surface of each Chalice, saying,*

O LORD God, be pleased to consecrate and
hallow this Chalice by this anointing, and by
our bene✠diction in Christ Jesus our Lord: Who
with thee in the unity of the Holy Spirit, liveth and
reigneth God, world without end. *Amen.*

*Laying aside his mitre, he says, over the Sacred
Vessels,*

℣. The Lord be with you.
℟. And with thy spirit.

Let us pray.

A LMIGHTY and everlasting God, we beseech thee
to pour the aid of thy blessing upon our hands,
that by our bene✠diction these vessels may be hallowed as a new sepulchre for the Body and Blood of
our Lord Jesus Christ, by the grace of thy Holy
Spirit. Through the same Christ our Lord. *Amen.*

*Afterward, the Priest shall cleanse the Sacred Vessels
with a small piece of bread, and then he shall cleanse
them well; and the bread crumb, etc., shall be cast into
the fire, or into the piscina.*

*A Priest who has been delegated to perform this
Consecration uses the foregoing rite, vested in surplice
and white stole.*

ADDITIONAL BLESSINGS

THE BLESSING OF A BIBLE

℣. Our help is in the Name of the Lord.

℟. Who hath made heaven and earth.

℣. O Lord hear my prayer.

℟. And let my cry come unto thee.

℣. The Lord be with you.

℟. And with thy spirit.

Let us pray.

O GOD, who hast given us thy holy Word to be a lantern unto our feet, and a light unto our paths: bl☩ess, we beseech thee, this copy of the Holy Scriptures; enlighten the hearts and minds of all who shall read therein, that they (*and those who hear*) may come to know him who is the way, the truth, and the life, even Jesus Christ thy Son our Lord. Who with thee, in the unity of the Holy Spirit, liveth and reigneth God, world without end. *Amen.*

If the Bible is to be used at the lectern, the Priest may cense it in the usual manner. And he may add,

Let us pray.

B LESSED Lord, who hast caused all holy Scriptures to be written for our learning; Grant that we may in such wise hear them, read, mark, learn and inwardly digest them, that by patience and comfort of thy holy Word, we may embrace, and ever hold fast, the blessed hope of everlasting life, which thou hast given us in our Saviour Jesus Christ. *Amen.*

THE BLESSING OF A CONFESSIONAL

℣. If we confess our sins.

℟. God is faithful and just to forgive our sins.

℣. Our help is in the Name of the Lord.

℞. Who hath made heaven and earth.

℣ The Lord be with you.

℞. And with thy spirit.

Let us pray.

O LORD Jesus Christ, who saidst unto thine Apostles, whosoever sins ye remit, they are remitted unto them; and whosoever sins ye retain they are retained: we pray thee to bl✝ess this confessional for the ministry of reconciliation; look mercifully upon thy servants who shall here confess their sins, that being filled with true contrition, they may have thy gift of absolution, and hereafter live according to thy law. Who with God the Father, in the unity of the Holy Spirit, livest and reignest God, world without end. *Amen.*

He may sprinkle it with holy water. Then he may add,

Let us pray for all who shall confess their sins in this place.

O LORD, we beseech thee, mercifully hear our prayers, and spare all those who confess their sins unto thee: that they, whose consciences by sin are accused, by thy merciful pardon may be absolved. Through Christ our Lord. *Amen.*

THE BLESSING OF A FONT

℣. Our help is in the Name of the Lord.

℞. Who hath made heaven and earth.

Psalm 46. *Deus noster refugium*

G OD is our hope and strength, ⋆ a very present help in trouble.

Therefore will we not fear, though the earth be moved, ★ and though the hills be carried into the midst of the sea;

Though the waters thereof rage and swell, ★ and though the mountains shake at the tempest of the same.

There is a river, the streams whereof make glad the city of God; ★ the holy place of the tabernacle of the Most Highest.

God is in the midst of her, therefore shall she not be removed; ★ God shall help her, and that right early.

The nations make much ado, and the kingdoms are moved; ★ but God hath showed his voice, and the earth shall melt away.

The Lord of hosts is with us; ★ the God of Jacob is our refuge.

O come hither, and behold the works of the Lord, ★ what destruction he hath brought upon the earth.

He maketh wars to cease in all the world; ★ he breaketh the bow, and knappeth the spear in sunder, and burneth the chariots in the fire.

Be still then, and know that I am God: ★ I will be exalted among the nations, and I will be exalted in the earth.

The Lord of hosts is with us; ★ the God of Jacob is our refuge.

Glory be to the Father, and to the Son, ★ and to the Holy Ghost;

As it was in the beginning, is now, and ever shall be, ★ world without end. Amen.

℣. Thou shalt purge me with hyssop O Lord, and I shall be clean.

℟. Thou shalt wash me, and I shall be whiter than snow.

℣. The Lord be with you.

℟. And with thy spirit.

Let us pray.

O GOD, who hast given us thine only begotten Son to be the way, the truth, and the life to all who believe in thee: graciously hearken to the prayers of thy servants, and vouchsafe to bless, hal⊹low and consecrate this font; and grant that whosoever shall be baptized therein may receive forgiveness of sin, and be made an heir of everlasting salvation. Through the same Christ our Lord. *Amen.*

Here the font may be sprinkled with holy water and censed. Then the Priest may add,

Let us pray.

REGARD, O Lord, the supplications of thy servants, and grant that whosoever in this house shall be received into the congregation of Christ's flock, may be sanctified by the Holy Ghost, and may continue Christ's faithful soldier and servant unto his life's end. Through the same thy Son Jesus Christ our Lord, who with thee, in the unity of the same Holy Ghost, liveth and reigneth God, world without end. *Amen.*

If there is a choir, the psalm may appropriately be sung.

THE BLESSING AND DISTRIBUTION OF MISSIONARY OFFERING BOXES

On Quinquagesima Sunday, or such other day as may be appointed, the Priest may bless Missionary Offering Boxes before they are distributed to the people.

The Offering Boxes to be blessed should be placed on a table in the midst of the Sanctuary, where it can be seen by the people.

The Priest stands behind the table, facing the people.

℣. **Our help is in the Name of the Lord.**
℟. **Who hath made heaven and earth.**
℣. **The Lord be with you.**
℟. **And with thy spirit.**

Let us pray.

O LORD Jesus Christ, who dost command us thy servants to proclaim thy Gospel unto the uttermost parts of the earth: we humbly pray thee to bl-✠-ess these offering boxes which thy servants are now to receive. Grant them grace, that they may give unto thee with generous hearts, and know the joy of thy redeeming love. Who with God the Father, in the unity of the Holy Spirit, livest and reignest God, world without end. *Amen.*

Here the Priest may sprinkle them with holy water, if it be the custom of the place.

The people kneel at the Altar Rail to receive their boxes. The Priest who distributes them says,

GO ye into all the world, and preach the Gospel to every creature.

Then shall the Priest say,

℣. **The Lord be with you.**
℟. **And with thy spirit.**

Let us pray for the missionary work of the Church.

O GOD, who hast made of one blood all nations of men for to dwell on the face of the whole earth, and didst send thy blessed Son to preach peace to them that are far off and to them that are nigh; Grant that all men everywhere may seek after thee and find thee. Bring the nations into thy fold, pour out thy Spirit upon all flesh, and hasten thy kingdom; through the same thy Son Jesus Christ our Lord. *Amen.*

THE BLESSING OF A LIBRARY

℣. Our help is in the Name of the Lord.
℟. Who hath made heaven and earth.
℣. The Lord be with you.
℟. And with thy spirit.

Let us pray.

O GOD, who art the Lord of all wisdom and knowledge: graciously bestow thy bl✠essing upon this library; grant that it may be preserved from fire and other perils, and be fittingly increased from day to day. May all who come here to serve in this library or to pursue their studies herein ever advance as well in the knowledge of things human and divine as, above all, in the love of thee. Through Christ our Lord. *Amen.*

THE BLESSING OF A SCHOOL

On entering the Priest sprinkles the rooms with holy water, saying,

℣. Peace be to this house.
℟. And to all that dwell in it.

Then in the principal room:

℣. Our help is in the Name of the Lord.

℟. Who hath made heaven and earth.

℣. The Lord be with you.

℟. And with thy spirit.

Let us pray.

O LORD Jesus Christ, who didst command thine Apostles that into whatsoever house they might enter they should pray for peace upon it: we beseech thee to sanc✠tify through our ministry this house devoted to the education of thy children; pour upon it the abundance of thy bl✠essing and thy peace, and may salvation come to them at thy entering herein, as it came to the house of Zaccheus. Give thy holy Angels charge to watch over it, and to drive far from it every power of the enemy; fill those who teach herein with the spirit of wisdom, of understanding, and of thy holy fear; guide with thy heavenly grace those who learn, that what they are duly taught they may lay hold of with their minds, retain in their hearts, and show forth in their lives; and may all who enter or dwell herein be so pleasing unto thee by virtuous deeds that they may be found worthy in due time to be received into eternal habitations in the heavens. Through thee, O Jesus Christ, Saviour of the world, who livest and reignest world without end. *Amen.*

If a new school building is to be solemnly blessed, the Priest may wear a white stole and cope. Clergy, teachers, scholars, and others should assemble outside; after the ℣. Peace be to this house, and its ℟,. the Priest sprinkles the outer walls with holy water. Meanwhile the Asperges me, *page 209, is sung.*

Entering, he proceeds as above, all gathering in the principal room; after the prayer this is sprinkled and censed. The Priest may then continue:

℣. The Lord be with you.
℟. And with thy spirit.

Let us pray.

VISIT, we beseech thee, O Lord, this habitation, and drive far from it all snares of the enemy: let thy holy Angels dwell herein to preserve in peace those who teach and those who learn, and let thy blessing be ever upon them. Through Christ our Lord. *Amen.*

BL✠ESS, O Lord, this house, that here may abide health, purity, victory, strength, humility, goodness, meekness, fulfilment of the law, and giving of thanks to God the Father, the Son, and the Holy Ghost. May this blessing remain upon this house and this place; and may the seven-fold grace of the Holy Spirit descend upon all who shall abide herein. Through the same Christ our Lord. *Amen.*

Other appropriate prayers may be added; if a crucifix or a figure of our Lord or a Saint is to be placed in this room, it may be blessed at this same time.

The Priest may conclude the service with this blessing:

THE blessing of God Almighty, the Father, the ✠ Son, and the Holy Ghost, be upon this house, and all who dwell herein, now and evermore. *Amen.*

If convenient, all should proceed to the Chapel, or to a neighboring Church for the Mass of the day.

THE BLESSING OF A BOOKSTORE
AND PRINTING PRESS

Standing at the door, the Priest says,

D IRECT us, O Lord, in all our doings, with thy most gracious favour, and further us with thy continual help; that in all our works begun, continued, and ended in thee, we may glorify thy holy Name, and finally, by thy mercy, obtain everlasting life; through Jesus Christ our Lord. *Amen.*

Entering, he says,

℣. Peace be to this house.
℞. And to all that dwell in it.

Then, saying the antiphon,

Thou shalt purge me with hyssop O Lord, and I shall be clean: thou shalt wash me, and I shall be whiter than snow,

He sprinkles the various rooms with holy water. When he arrives at the principal one he stops and says,

℣. Our help is in the Name of the Lord.
℞. Who hath made heaven and earth.
℣. The Lord be with you.
℞. And with thy spirit.

Let us pray.

O LORD Jesus Christ, who saidst unto thine Apostles, Into whatsoever house ye enter, salute it, saying, Peace be to this house: may that peace, we beseech thee, come upon this house and building devoted to the printing (*or* distribution) of books. Vouchsafe, O Lord, to deliver all who labor here from all distress of body and soul; fill all who in any way may take part in this enterprise with the spirit of wisdom, counsel, and strength, and inspire them with the spirit of thy holy fear, that, loyally following the precepts of thy Church they may be able worthily to serve both thee and their neighbors. O good Jesus, who art the Way, the Truth, and the Life, do thou bl✠ess this place, and grant that all who dwell here may, at the intercession of thy glorious and ever-Virgin Mother Mary, joyfully attain to the crown of glory that fadeth not away. Who livest and reignest God, world without end. *Amen.*

Then he blesses the tools and machines, saying,

Let us pray.

O LORD God, the only fountain of all wisdom, who hast vouchsafed so to illuminate the minds of men that they have discovered new devices for multiplying the written word: bl✠ess we beseech thee, *these machines;* and grant that, aided by the books which they produce for our benefit, we may in and above all things learn the true wisdom which leadeth unto eternal life. Through Christ our Lord. *Amen.*

And they are sprinkled with holy water. When this is finished, the Priest says,

℣. The Lord be with you.
℟. And with thy spirit.

Let us pray.

GRACIOUSLY hear us, O Lord holy, Father Almighty, everlasting God: and send thy holy Angel from heaven to guard, cherish, protect, visit,

and defend all who dwell in this habitation. Through Christ our Lord. *Amen.*

Either prayer of blessing may be used alone as occasion may require.

THE BLESSING OF A SPACE CRAFT

℣. Our help is in the Name of the Lord.
℟. Who hath made heaven and earth.
℣. Thou art God from everlasting.
℟. And world without end.
℣. O Lord, hear my prayer.
℟. And let my cry come unto thee.
℣. The Lord be with you.
℟. And with thy spirit.

Let us pray.

O GOD, the King and Lord of all, who hast created all things in the universe: graciously hear our prayers, and bl✠ess this craft now prepared for the journeys of thy servants in space. Be present with those who are charged with its navigation, protect them in all perils; prosper them in their course, and bring them to their destination; and at length conduct them in safety to the haven where they would be. Through thy Son, Jesus Christ our Lord, who with thee, in the unity of the Holy Spirit, liveth and reigneth God, world without end. *Amen.*

Various Prayers

Particular collections of prayers, drawn from the Books of Common Prayer and other approved sources, will be found in this book, as noted below.

Additional Collects and Prayers, complementary to those of the American Book of Common Prayer, will be found in the pages immediately following.

SACRISTY PRAYERS

1 Before Celebrating
2 After Celebrating
3 Before Morning or Evening Prayer
4 After Morning or Evening Prayer
5 With the Choir Before Service
6 With the Choir After Service

SEASONAL PRAYERS

7 An Advent Prayer
8 A Christmastide Prayer
9 At the New Year
10 On New Year's Day
11 For the Coming Year
12 For Epiphanytide
13 For Lent
14 For Passiontide
15 For Eastertide
16 Rogation Days: For Agriculture
17 Rogation Days: For the Harvest of the Waters
18 Rogation Days: For Industries
19 For Ascensiontide
20 For Whitsuntide
21 For Trinity Sunday
22 In the Ember Weeks

254

23 For Saints Days
24 At the Opening of the Law Courts

FOR THE CHURCH AND HER WORK

25 For the Church
26 For the Unity of the Church
27 For the Presiding Bishop
28 For the House of Bishops
29 For the Bishop of the Diocese
30 For the General or Diocesan Convention
31 For Unbaptized Inquirers and Catechumens
32 For Confirmation Candidates
33 For the Increase of the Ministry
34 For Theological Seminaries
35 For the Spread of the Gospel
36 For Home Missions
37 For Missionaries in Other Lands
38 For the Jews
39 For the Moslems and All Who Know Not Christ
40 For the Heathen
41 For Religious Communities
42 For Church Workers
43 For Meetings of Church Organizations
44 For the Right Observance of Sunday

THE STATE

45 For our Country
46 For Those in Authority
47 For the Legislature or Congress
48 For the Peace of the World
49 For the United Nations
50 In Time of War
51 For the Armed Forces
52 At the Time of an Election
53 In Time of Industrial Strife
54 For Christian Citizenship

CHRISTIAN FAMILY LIFE

55 For Christian Homes
56 For a Child's Home

SACRISTY PRAYERS

1 *Before Celebrating*

PURIFY our consciences, we beseech thee, O Lord, by thy visitation: that our Lord Jesus Christ thy Son, when he cometh, may find in us a mansion prepared for himself. Who with thee, in the unity of the Holy Spirit, liveth and reigneth God, world without end. *Amen.*

2 *After Celebrating*

MAY the homage of our service be pleasing unto thee, O Father Almighty; and grant that the sacrifice which we have offered unto thee for the welfare of the living and for the repose of the departed, may avail them and us for salvation unto life eternal. Through Christ our Lord. *Amen.*

3 *Before Matins or Evensong*

OPEN my mouth, O Lord, to bless thy holy Name: cleanse my heart from all vain, evil, and wandering thoughts; enlighten my understanding and kindle my affections, that I may pray this Office with attention and devotion, and so may be meet to be heard in the presence of thy divine Majesty. Through Christ our Lord. *Amen.*

4 *After Matins or Evensong*

UNTO the most holy and undivided Trinity, unto the sacred humanity of our crucified Lord Jesus Christ, be everlasting praise, honour and glory from every creature, and unto us the remission of all our sins, now and forever. *Amen.*

5 *With the Choir Before Service*

O LORD open thou our lips and purify our hearts, that we may reverently and devoutly take part in this service. Through Christ our Lord. *Amen.*

6 *With the Choir After Service*

GRANT, O Lord, that what we have said and sung with our lips we may believe in our hearts and practise in our lives. Through Christ our Lord. *Amen.*

SEASONAL PRAYERS

7 *An Advent Prayer*

GRANT, O Almighty God, that as thy blessed Son Jesus Christ at his first advent came to seek and to save that which was lost, so at his second and glorious appearing he may find in us the fruits of the redemption which he wrought; who liveth and reigneth, with thee and the Holy Spirit, one God, world without end. *Amen.*

8 *A Christmastide Prayer*

O GOD, who hast given us grace at this time to celebrate the birth of our Saviour Jesus Christ: We laud and magnify thy glorious Name for the countless blessings which he hath brought unto us; and we beseech thee to grant that we may ever set forth thy praise in joyful obedience to thy will; through the same Jesus Christ our Lord. *Amen.*

9 *At the New Year*

O IMMORTAL Lord God, who inhabitest eternity, and hast brought us to the beginning of another year: Pardon, we humbly beseech thee, our transgressions in the past, and graciously abide with us all the days of our life; guard and direct us in all trials and temptations, that by thy blessing we may grow in grace as we grow in years, and at the last may finish our course with joy; through Jesus Christ our Lord. *Amen.*

10 *On New Year's Day*

O SAVIOUR of the world, who as on this day wast called Jesus, according to the word of the Angel: Fulfil unto us, we beseech thee, the gracious promise of that holy Name, and, of thy great mercy, save thy people from their sins; who with the Father and the Holy Spirit livest and reignest, one God, world without end. *Amen.*

11 *For the Coming Year*

O THOU, who art ever the same: grant us grace so to pass through the coming year with faithful hearts, that in all things we may please thy loving eyes. Who livest and reignest, world without end. *Amen.*

12 *For Epiphanytide*

ALMIGHTY God, who at the baptism of thy blessed Son Jesus Christ in the river Jordan didst manifest his glorious Godhead: Grant, we beseech thee, that the brightness of his presence may shine in our hearts, and his glory be set forth in our lives; through the same Jesus Christ our Lord. *Amen.*

13 *For Lent*

O GOD, whose nature and property is ever to have mercy and to forgive: Receive our humble petitions; and though we be tied and bound with the chain of our sins, let the pitifulness of thy great mercy loose us; for the honour of our Mediator and Advoeate, Jesus Christ our Lord. *Amen.*

14 *For Passiontide*

O GOD, who by the cross and passion of thy Son Jesus Christ didst save and deliver mankind: Grant that by stedfast faith in the merits of that holy sacrifice we may find help and salvation, and may triumph in the power of his victory; through the same Jesus Christ our Lord. *Amen.*

15 *For Eastertide*

O LORD God Almighty, whose blessed Son our Saviour Jesus Christ did on the third day rise triumphant over death: Raise us, we beseech thee, from the death of sin unto the life of righteousness, that we may seek those things which are above, where he sitteth on thy right hand in glory; and this we beg for the sake of the same thy Son Jesus Christ our Lord. *Amen.*

16 *Rogation Days: For Agriculture*

O ALMIGHTY God, who hast created the earth for man, and man for thy glory: Mercifully hear the supplications of thy people, and be mindful of thy covenant; that the earth may yield her increase, and the good seed of thy word may bring forth abundantly, to the glory of thy holy Name; through Jesus Christ our Lord. *Amen.*

17 *Rogation Days: For the Harvest of the Waters*

O ALMIGHTY GOD, who madest the sea, and gavest all that moveth therein for the use of man: Bestow thy blessing, we beseech thee, on the harvest of the waters, that it may be abundant in its season; protect from every peril of the deep all fishermen and mariners, and grant that they may with thankful hearts acknowledge thee, who art Lord of the sea and of the dry land; through Jesus Christ our Lord. *Amen.*

18 *Rogation Days: For Industries*

O ALMIGHTY Father, who through thy Son Jesus Christ hast consecrated labour to the blessing of mankind: Prosper, we pray thee, the industries of this land (especially in this place); defend those who are engaged therein from all perils, and grant that they may rejoice in the fruits of thy bounty, and bless thee for thy loving-kindness; through the same Jesus Christ our Lord. *Amen.*

19 *For Ascensiontide*

ALMIGHTY God, whose blessed Son our Saviour Jesus Christ ascended far above all heavens that he might fill all things: Mercifully give us faith to perceive that according to his promise he abideth with his Church on earth, even unto the end of the world; through the same Jesus Christ our Lord. *Amen.*

20 *For Whitsuntide*

O ALMIGHTY God, who on the day of Pentecost didst send the Holy Ghost the Comforter to abide in thy Church unto the end: Bestow upon us and upon all thy faithful people his manifold gifts of grace, that with minds enlightened by his truth, and hearts purified by his presence, we may day by day be strengthened with power in the inward man; through Jesus Christ our Lord, who with thee and the same Spirit liveth and reigneth, one God, world without end. *Amen.*

21 *For Trinity Sunday*

O LORD God Almighty, Eternal, Immortal, Invisible, the mysteries of whose being are unsearchable: Accept, we beseech thee, our praises for the revelation which thou hast made of thyself, Father, Son, and Holy Spirit, three Persons, and one God; and mercifully grant, that ever holding fast this faith, we may magnify thy glorious Name; who livest and reignest, one God, world without end. *Amen.*

22 *In the Ember Weeks*

O ALMIGHTY God, look mercifully upon the world, redeemed by the blood of thy dear Son, and incline the hearts of all whom thou dost call to offer themselves for the sacred ministry of thy Church; that there may never be wanting a supply of fit persons to preach thy Word, and dispense thy holy Sacraments; through the same Jesus Christ our Lord. *Amen.*

23 *For Saints' Days*

O GOD the King of Saints, we praise and magnify thy holy Name for all thy servants who have finished their course in thy faith and fear: for the Blessed Virgin Mary, for the holy Patriarchs, Prophets, Apostles and Martyrs, and for all other thy righteous servants; and we beseech thee that, encouraged by their example, strengthened by their fellowship, and aided by their prayers, we may attain unto everlasting life; through the merits of thy Son Jesus Christ our Lord. *Amen.*

24 *At the Opening of the Law Courts*

WE pray thee, O Lord, for all courts of justice and the magistrates in all this land: that all, and every one of them, may serve truly in their several callings to thy glory, and the edifying and well-governing of thy people, remembering the account they shall be called upon to give at the last great day; through Jesus Christ our Lord. *Amen.*

FOR THE CHURCH AND HER WORK

25 *For the Church*

O GOD of unchangeable power and eternal light, look favourably upon thy whole Church, that wonderful and sacred mystery: and by the tranquil operation of thy perpetual providence carry out the work of man's salvation; that things which were cast down may be raised up, and that all things may come to perfection through him by whom all things were made, even Jesus Christ thy Son our Lord. *Amen.*

26 *For the Unity of the Church*

VOUCHSAFE, we beseech thee, Almighty God, to grant to all Christian people unity, peace and true concord, both visible and invisible; through Jesus Christ our Lord. *Amen.*

27 *For the Presiding Bishop*

O GOD, the Pastor and Ruler of all thy faithful people: look down in mercy upon thy servant *N.*, our Primate, whom thou hast set to preside over thy Church; and evermore guide, defend, comfort, sanctify and save him, and grant him by thy grace so to advance in word and good example, that he, with the flock committed to him, may attain to everlasting life; through Jesus Christ our Lord. *Amen.*

28 *For the House of Bishops*

O LORD God, the Father of lights and fountain of all wisdom, who in the days of the Apostles didst send thy Holy Spirit to direct the first Council of thy Church in Jerusalem: look mercifully upon thy Church in this land, and so bless our Bishops now (to be) assembled, that through their deliberations thy Church may be preserved in the true faith, and in godly discipline; through our Lord and Saviour Jesus Christ. *Amen.*

29 *For the Bishop of the Diocese*

O GOD, the Pastor and Ruler of all thy faithful people: look down in mercy upon thy servant *N.* our Bishop, to whom thou hast given charge over this Diocese of *N.*; and evermore guide, defend, sanctify and save him; and grant him by thy grace so to advance in word and good example, that he, with the flock committed to him, may attain to everlasting life; through Jesus Christ our Lord. *Amen.*

30 *For the General or Diocesan Convention*

G UIDE, we beseech thee, Almighty God, with the light of thy Holy Spirit, our Bishop(s), Clergy and Laity, in the General (*or* Diocesan) Convention, that they may wisely consult together for the good of thy Church and the glory of thy Name; through Jesus Christ our Lord. *Amen.*

31 *For Inquirers and Catechumens*

O GOD our Father, grant, we beseech thee, that all inquirers and catechumens may learn to know thy Son Jesus Christ, the forgiveness won by his death, and the power of his resurrection; that, coming to thy holy Baptism, they may be born again of water and the Spirit, and be made heirs of eternal salvation; through the same thy Son, our Saviour Jesus Christ. *Amen.*

32 *For Confirmation Candidates*

O MERCIFUL and gracious Lord, our heavenly Father, strengthen, we beseech thee, thy servants with the sevenfold gift of thy Holy Spirit, that those who are admitted to the fulness of Christian

grace may grow into the perfection of Christian
life; through the merits of thy Son, our Lord and
Saviour Jesus Christ. *Amen.*

33 *For the Increase of the Ministry*

O LORD Jesus Christ, whose servants Simon
Peter and Andrew his brother did at thy word
straightway leave their nets to become fishers of
men: Give thy grace, we humbly beseech thee, to
those whom thou dost call to the sacred ministry of
thy Church, that they may hear thy voice, and with
glad hearts obey thy word; who livest and reignest
with the Father and the Holy Spirit, one God, world
without end. *Amen.*

34 *For Theological Seminaries*

A LMIGHTY God, whose blessed Son called the
twelve Apostles and taught them the mysteries
of the kingdom of heaven: bless, we beseech thee,
those who are preparing for the sacred ministry of
thy Church, and those appointed to teach and guide
them; that, illuminated with a true understanding
of thy Word and Sacraments, and growing in holiness
of life, they may be made able ministers of the New
Covenant, and may advance thy glory and the salvation of thy elect servants; through the same Jesus
Christ our Lord. *Amen.*

35 *For the Spread of the Gospel*

O GOD, our heavenly Father, who didst manifest
thy love by sending thine only-begotten Son
into the world that all might live through him: pour
thy Spirit upon thy Church that it may fulfil his
command to preach the Gospel to every creature;
send forth, we beseech thee, labourers into thy

harvest; defend them in all dangers and temptations; and hasten the time when the fulness of the Gentiles shall be gathered in, and all Israel shall be saved; through the same thy Son Jesus Christ our Lord. *Amen.*

36 *For Home Missions*

O LORD Jesus Christ, thou good Shepherd of the sheep, who came to seek and to save that which was lost: We beseech thee to be present in thy power with the Missions of thy Church in our land. Show forth thy compassion to the helpless, enlighten the ignorant, succour those in peril, and bring home the wanderers in safety to thy fold; who livest and reignest with the Father and the Holy Spirit, one God, world without end. *Amen.*

37 *For Missionaries in Other Lands*

O GOD our Saviour, who willest that all men should be saved and come to the knowledge of the truth: Prosper, we pray thee, our brethren who labour in other lands, (especially *those* for whom our prayers are desired). Protect them in all perils; support them in loneliness and in the hour of trial; give them grace to bear faithful witness unto thee; and endue them with burning zeal and love, that they may turn many to righteousness, and finally obtain a crown of glory; through Jesus Christ our Lord. *Amen.*

38 *For the Jews*

O LORD God of Abraham, look upon thine everlasting covenant, and hear the prayers which we offer unto thee for thine own people, that acknowledging the light of thy truth, which is Christ, they may come unto thee; through him who is the true Messiah, Jesus Christ thy Son our Lord, who with thee, in the unity of the Holy Spirit, liveth and reigneth God, world without end. *Amen.*

39 *For the Moslems and All Who Know Not Christ*

ALMIGHTY God, our heavenly Father, who in thy goodness hast caused the light of the Gospel to shine in the world: Enlighten the Moslems with the knowledge of thy truth; and grant that all who worship thee the one God may come to know thy Son, Jesus Christ our Lord; who with thee, in the unity of the Holy Spirit, liveth and reigneth God, world without end. *Amen.*

40 *For the Heathen*

O GOD of all the nations of the earth, remember the multitudes of the heathen, who have not known thee; and grant that by the prayers and labours of thy holy Church they may be delivered from all superstition and unbelief, and brought to worship thee; through him whom thou hast sent to be the Resurrection and the Life of all men, thy Son Jesus Christ our Lord. *Amen.*

41 *For Religious Communities*

O LORD Jesus Christ, who hast taught us that he who loseth his life for thy sake shall find it: Bestow, we pray thee, thine abundant blessings upon those who have left all, and dedicated themselves to thy service, under vows of poverty, chastity and obedience; that they may neither look back, nor stray from thy way, but so steadfastly persevere in thy service, that in the end they may receive the crown of everlasting life. Through the same thy Son, Jesus Christ our Lord. *Amen.*

42 *For Church Workers*

ALMIGHTY and everlasting God, by whose
Spirit the whole body of the Church is governed
and sanctified: receive our supplications and prayers,
which we offer before thee for all estates of men in
thy holy Church, that every member of the same, in
his vocation and ministry, may truly and godly
serve thee; through our Lord and Saviour Jesus
Christ. *Amen.*

43 *For Meetings of Church Organizations*

ALMIGHTY and everlasting God, from whom
cometh wisdom and understanding: be present,
we beseech thee. in this meeting of thy servants; and
grant that they, seeking only thy honour and glory,
may be guided in all their consultations to perceive
the more excellent way, and may have grace and
strength to follow the same; through Jesus Christ
our Lord. *Amen.*

44 *For the Right Observance of Sunday*

ALMIGHTY God, who through thy Church hast
consecrated the first day of the week to be a
perpetual memorial of thy Son's resurrection: teach
us so to reverence this holy day, that refreshed and
renewed by thy Word and Sacrament, we may serve
thee faithfully all our days; through the same Jesus
Christ our Lord. *Amen.*

THE STATE

45 *For Our Country*

LORD of all power and might, from whom
cometh every good and perfect gift: pour out
thy blessing upon our land, that we may have grace

to use thy rich gifts according to thy holy will; and strengthen us to seek peace and justice for all mankind. Through Christ our Lord. *Amen.*

46 *For Those in Authority*

O GOD, we beseech thee to assist the rulers of our land with thy continual blessing: that they, worthily exercising the power which thou hast given them, may truly and righteously govern the people committed to their charge; through Jesus Christ our Lord. *Amen.*

47 *For the Legislature*

O GOD, the fountain of all wisdom, whose statutes are good and gracious, and whose law is truth: we beseech thee so to guide and bless our Congress (*or* Legislature), that it may ordain for our governance only such things as please thee, to the glory of thy Name and the welfare of thy people; through Jesus Christ our Lord. *Amen.*

48 *For the Peace of the World*

A LMIGHTY God, from whom all thoughts of truth and of peace proceed: Kindle, we pray thee, in the hearts of all men the true love of peace; and guide with thy heavenly wisdom those who take counsel for the nations of the earth; that in tranquility thy kingdom may go forward, till the earth is filled with the knowledge of thy love; through Jesus Christ our Lord. *Amen.*

49 *For the United Nations*

A LMIGHTY God, the King of kings and Lord of lords: guide, we beseech thee, the nations of the world into the way of justice and truth, and establish among them that peace which is the fruit of righteousness; through him in whose obedience alone is true righteousness and peace, our Lord and Saviour Jesus Christ. *Amen.*

50 *In Time of War*

O ALMIGHTY God, who art a most strong tower to all who put their trust in thee: Be now and evermore our defence; grant us victory, if it be thy will; look in pity upon the wounded and the prisoners; cheer the anxious; comfort the bereaved; succour the dying; have mercy upon the fallen; and hasten the time when war shall cease in all the world; through Jesus Christ our Lord. *Amen.*

51 *For the Armed Forces*

O LORD God of hosts, stretch forth thine almighty power to strengthen and protect those who are serving in the armed forces of our country: shelter them in the day of battle; keep them safe from all evil; endue them ever with loyalty and courage; that in all things they may serve as seeing thee who art invisible; through Jesus Christ our Lord. *Amen.*

52 *At the Time of an Election*

O LORD, we beg thee to govern the minds of all who are called at this time to choose faithful persons to serve in the government of this land (*or as need may require*): that they may exercise their choice as in thy sight, for the welfare of all our people; through Jesus Christ our Lord. *Amen.*

53 *In Time of Industrial Strife*

O GOD, who willest that men should live and work together as brethren: we beseech thee to remove the spirit of strife and selfishness from those who are now at variance; that seeking only what is just they may ever abide in brotherly union and concord, to their own well-being and the good of all mankind; through Jesus Christ our Lord. *Amen.*

54 *For Christian Citizenship*

WE beseech thee, O Lord, mercifully to behold the people of this land who are called after thy holy Name; and grant that we may ever walk worthy of our Christian profession. Laying aside our divisions, may we be united in heart and mind to bear the burdens which are laid upon us. Help us to respond to the call of our country according to our several powers; put far from us selfish indifference to the needs of others; and give us grace to fulfil our daily duties with sober diligence. Keep us from all uncharitableness in word or deed; and enable us by patient continuance in well-doing to glorify thy Name; through Jesus Christ our Lord. *Amen.*

CHRISTIAN FAMILY LIFE

55 *For Christian Homes*

VISIT, we beseech thee, O Lord, our homes, and drive far from them all snares of the enemy: let thy holy Angels dwell therein to preserve us in peace, and let thy blessing be ever upon us; through Jesus Christ our Lord. *Amen.*

56 *For a Child's Home*

ALMIGHTY God, our heavenly Father, whose blessed Son did share at Nazareth the life of an earthly home: Bless, we beseech thee, the home of this Child; and grant wisdom and understanding to all who have the care of *him*, that *he* may grow

up in thy constant fear and love; through the same
thy Son Jesus Christ our Lord. *Amen.*

57 *For Parents*

O GOD, our heavenly Father, who hast blessed
thy servants with the gift of a child: Grant,
we beseech thee, that they may show their love and
thankfulness to thee in so ordering their home, that
by the example of their life and teaching they may
guide their child in the way of righteousness, and
with *him* be partakers with thy saints in the life to
come; through Jesus Christ our Lord. *Amen.*

58 *For a Birthday*

O GOD, in whom we live and move and have our
being: we give thee hearty thanks for the
preservation of thy servant from the beginning of
his life until this day. Grant *him*, we humbly pray,
that as *he* grows in age so may *he* also grow in
grace; through Jesus Christ our Lord. *Amen.*

59 *For Children*

A LMIGHTY God, heavenly Father, who hast
blessed us with the joy and care of children:
Give us light and strength so to train them that they
may love whatsoever things are true, and pure, and
lovely, and of good report; following the example
of their Saviour, Jesus Christ. *Amen.*

FOR EDUCATION

60 *For Universities, Colleges and Schools*

A LMIGHTY God, we beseech thee with thy
gracious favour to behold our Universities,
Colleges and Schools, that knowledge may be increased among us, and all good learning flourish

and abound. Bless all who teach and all who learn;
and grant that in humility of heart they may ever
look unto thee, who art the fountain of all wisdom;
through Jesus Christ our Lord. *Amen.*

61 *For Teachers*

ALMIGHTY Father, who didst send thine only
Son, that through him all men might be saved:
So consecrate the lives of those whom thou dost
call to teach, that, being themselves led by thee,
they may lead their pupils in the paths of everlasting
life; through the same our Lord and Saviour Jesus
Christ. *Amen.*

62 *For Teachers and Learners*

ALMIGHTY God, our heavenly Father, who
hast committed to thy holy Church the care
and nurture of thy children: Enlighten with thy
wisdom those who teach and those who learn; that,
rejoicing in the knowledge of thy truth, they may
worship thee and serve thee all the days of their life;
through Jesus Christ our Lord. *Amen.*

63 *For Learners*

O LORD Jesus Christ, who as a child didst
learn, and didst grow in wisdom: Grant us so
to learn thy holy Word, that we may walk in thy
ways and daily grow more like unto thee; who livest
and reignest with the Father and the Holy Ghost,
one God, world without end. *Amen.*

64 *Before an Athletic Contest*

O ALMIGHTY God, who alone art the final
judge of life's great race: be with this our *N.*
team in its contest of sporting skill, and grant that

should we win we may accept our victory humbly; or
should we be defeated we may take our loss graciously; through Jesus Christ our Lord. *Amen.*

TRAVELLERS AND THE ABSENT

65 *For Absent Friends and Relatives*

O LORD our God, who art in every place: we
thank thee that no space or distance can
separate us from thee, and that those who are
absent from each other are still present with thee.
Have in thy holy keeping those from whom we are
now separated, and grant that both they and we, by
drawing nearer to thee, may be drawn nearer to
each other; through Jesus Christ our Lord. *Amen.*

66 *For Travellers (general)*

O GOD, who art not far from each one of us:
be near to all who travel by land, sea, or air;
lighten their way with the grace of thy presence,
preserve them in all dangers and in all temptations,
direct their paths in tranquility, and bring them in
health and safety to their journey's end; through
Jesus Christ our Lord. *Amen.*

67 *For Travellers by Sea*

O ALMIGHTY God, whose way is in the sea,
and whose paths are in great waters: be present,
we beseech thee, with our brethren in the manifold
dangers of the deep; protect them from all its perils;
prosper them in their course; and in safety bring
them to the haven where they would be, with a grateful sense of thy mercies; Through Jesus Christ our
Lord. *Amen.*

68 *For Travellers by Air*

ALMIGHTY God, who makest the clouds thy chariot, and walkest upon the wings of the wind: be with all who travel by air, that trusting to thy protection, they may come securely to their journey's end; through Jesus Christ our Lord. *Amen.*

69 *For Explorers in Outer Space*

O GOD, who hast created the heavens and the earth: guide and preserve those who penetrate the vastness of outer space; and grant that we who learn from their explorations may come to perceive the majesty of thy creation, and turn to thee for grace to use that knowledge for the good of all mankind. Through Jesus Christ our Lord. *Amen.*

OTHER

70 *For Hospitals*

ALMIGHTY God, whose blessed Son Jesus Christ went about healing all manner of sickness and distress: continue, we beseech thee, his gracious work among us in all our hospitals (and especially in *N.*); comfort and heal those who suffer; grant wisdom and skill to physicians, surgeons, nurses and technicians, together with gentleness and patience. Prosper their work with thy continual blessing; through the same Jesus Christ our Lord. *Amen.*

71 *For Nursing Homes*

O LORD Jesus Christ, who hast compassion upon all whom thou hast made: mercifully behold the nursing homes of our land, and those who live and work therein (especially . . .). Give them an increase of faith, hope and charity; give them sure confidence in thy never-failing care and love; and grant them all things needful, both for this life and that which is to come. Who with the Father, in the unity of the Holy Spirit, livest and reignest God, world without end. *Amen.*

72 *For Fire Fighters and Police*

When this prayer is used at a gathering of Fire Fighters, the reference to Police may be omitted; at a gathering of Police the reference to Fire Fighters may be omitted.

WE beseech thee, Almighty God, to pour thy blessing upon the Fire Fighters and the Police of our land: strengthen and preserve them in every danger; that they, who protect our lives and property while they faithfully perform their duties, may so serve thee here that they fail not finally to attain thy heavenly promises. Through Jesus Christ our Lord. *Amen.*

73 *For Worker Priests and Deacons*

O LORD Jesus Christ, who saidst unto thine Apostles, I am among you as he that serveth: give thy blessing to the Worker Priests and Deacons of thy Church; that as blessed Paul the Apostle supported himself by the work of his hands while preaching the Word and ministering the Sacraments, so these thy servants in their special vocation may seek thine own who have not known thee, and those who have fallen away from thee; and finding them may bring thine own unto thee, true Bishop and Shepherd of our souls. Who livest and reignest, world without end. *Amen.*

Graces for Ecumenical and Other Occasions

BL✠ESS, O Father, thy gifts to our use and us to thy service; for Christ's sake. *Amen.*

GIVE us grateful hearts, our Father, for all thy mercies, and make us mindful of the needs of others; through Jesus Christ our Lord. *Amen.*

BLESS us, O Lord, and these ✠ thy gifts, of which through thy bounty we are about to partake. Through Christ our Lord. *Amen.*

WE give thanks to thee, O Almighty God, for all thy benefits. Who livest and reignest, world without end. *Amen.*

BLESSED be the Lord in his gifts, and holy in all his works. Who liveth and reigneth, world without end. *Amen.*

BLESSED art thou, O Lord our God, King of the universe, who bringest forth bread from the earth. *Amen.*

BLESSED art thou, O Lord our God, King of the universe, who dost create the fruit of the vine. *Amen.*

THE King of eternal glory make us partakers of his heavenly table. *Amen.*

THE King of eternal glory bring us to the supper of eternal life. *Amen.*

FOR these, and all his other gifts, may God's holy Name be praised and blessed. *Amen.*

BE present at our table, Lord, Be here and everywhere adored; These mercies bless, and grant that we May feast in Paradise with thee. *Amen.*

277

BLESSINGS FOR ECUMENICAL AND OTHER OCCASIONS

THE Blessing of God Almighty, the Father, the ✠ Son, and the Holy Ghost, be upon you, and remain with you for ever. *Amen.*

THE Peace of God, which passeth all understanding, keep your hearts and minds in the knowledge and love of God, and of his Son Jesus Christ our Lord: And the Blessing of God Almighty, the Father, the ✠ Son, and the Holy Ghost, be amongst you, and remain with you always. *Amen.*

UNTO God's gracious mercy and protection we commit you. The Lord bless you and keep you. The Lord make his face to shine upon you and be gracious unto you. The Lord lift up his countenance upon you, and give you peace, both now and evermore. *Amen.*

THE God of peace, who brought again from the dead our Lord Jesus Christ, the great Shepherd of the sheep, through the blood of the everlasting covenant; Make you perfect in every good work to do his will, working in you that which is well pleasing in his sight; through Jesus Christ, to whom be glory for ever and ever. *Amen.*

THE Lord bless you and keep you: the Lord make his face to shine upon you, and be gracious unto you: the Lord lift up his countenance upon you, and give you peace, now and evermore. *Amen.*

278

A Commemoration of the Saints and Faithful Departed

Let us commemorate before God the saints and faithful departed.

℣. The righteous live for evermore;
℟. Their reward also is with the Lord.

O GOD the King of Saints, we praise and magnify thy holy Name for all thy servants who have finished their course in thy faith and fear, for the Blessed Virgin Mary, for the holy Patriarchs, Prophets, Apostles, and Martyrs, and for all other thy righteous servants; and we beseech thee that, encouraged by their example, strengthened by their fellowship, and aided by their prayers, we may attain unto everlasting life; through the merits of thy Son Jesus Christ our Lord. *Amen.*

—*The Scottish Book of Common Prayer*

279

INDEXES

INDEXES

NUMERICAL INDEX OF PSALMS

INDEX OF HYMNS AND CANTICLES

INDEX OF LESSONS

ALPHABETICAL INDEX OF BLESSINGS

The General Rubric relating to the use of Blessings will be found on page 125.

INDEX OF VARIOUS PRAYERS

SUBJECT INDEX

Manuscript Additions